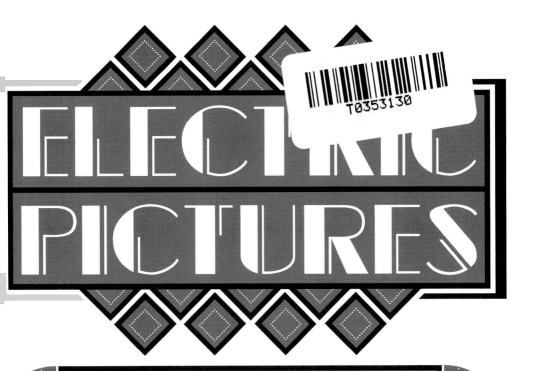

ELECTRIC PICTURES

A GUIDE TO THE FILMS, FILM-MAKERS & CINEMAS

OF

WORTHING & SHOREHAM

ELLEN CHESHIRE & JAMES CLARKE

The History Press

T0353130

First published 2017

The History Press
The Mill, Brimscombe Port
Stroud, Gloucestershire, GL5 2QG
www.thehistorypress.co.uk

British Library Cataloguing in Publication Data.
A catalogue record for this book is available from the British Library.

ISBN 978 0 7509 8141 5

Typesetting and origination by The History Press
Printed and bound in Great Britain by TJ International Ltd

CONTENTS

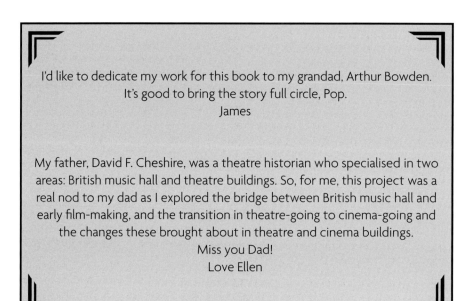

I'd like to dedicate my work for this book to my grandad, Arthur Bowden.
It's good to bring the story full circle, Pop.
James

My father, David F. Cheshire, was a theatre historian who specialised in two areas: British music hall and theatre buildings. So, for me, this project was a real nod to my dad as I explored the bridge between British music hall and early film-making, and the transition in theatre-going to cinema-going and the changes these brought about in theatre and cinema buildings.
Miss you Dad!
Love Ellen

ABOUT THE AUTHORS

ELLEN CHESHIRE is a freelance film researcher, writer and lecturer. She has published books on biopics (for Columbia University Press), Ang Lee and Jane Campion (for Supernova Books), Audrey Hepburn and the Coen Brothers (for Pocket Essentials), and has contributed chapters to books on James Bond and Charlie Chaplin (for Taschen Books), silent film and counterculture (for Supernova Books), fantasy films (for MS Publications) and war movies (for Ian Allen). She has lectured in film and media at the University of Chichester and Chichester College. In 2016 she was Film Historian for Worthing WOW's Heritage Lottery funded project celebrating 120 years of film in Sussex.

JAMES CLARKE is a freelance writer and lecturer. His books include *The Virgin Film Guide: War Films* and *Movie Movements: Films that Changed the World of Cinema* and he has contributed to *The Rough Guide to Film*. He has worked extensively in community film-making and film education and several of his short film projects have played at national and international film festivals. He writes regularly for the magazines *3DArtist* and *SciFi Now*. His writing has also been published by *Resurgence* and *Country Walking* magazines. James has taught at a number of universities, including the Universities of Gloucestershire and Warwick. James is currently co-writing a feature-film screenplay.

ACKNOWLEDGEMENTS

There are many people to thank. Firstly, thank you to Melody Bridges, Worthing WOW, The History Press and Heritage Lottery Fund for allowing us to take this wonderful journey through 120 years of film-making and cinema-going in Worthing and Shoreham.

Helping us along the way have been film historians Frank Gray at Screen Archive South East, Kevin Brownlow, Tony Fletcher, Martin Humphires and Ronald Grant. From a local history perspective, thanks go to Emma O'Connor, curator at Sussex Past/Marlipins Museum, Gary Baines and Sharon Penfold at Shoreham Fort, Brian Meetens, Ian Merriwoode, Roger Bateman, Kelly Mikula at Sussex Film Office, Stefan Sykes at Worthing Film Club and the team at Ropetackle in Shoreham.

Special thanks go to David Leland for speaking to James about his memories of making *Wish You Were Here* and to Sir Sydney Samuelson for talking with Ellen, and to Gillian Gregg for allowing us to use images from her archives.

Photographs: thanks go to everyone who helped to source and share some incredible images. We have added a credit alongside each photograph. We have endeavoured to find the copyright holder for all images but apologise to anyone we may have inadvertently missed out.

FOREWORD

I am appalled by my ignorance. Having devoted most of my life to working in the film and television industry, I discover I have been ignorant of a significant portion of British cinematic history. That is, until I read this thoroughly entertaining book, *Electric Pictures*.

The first surprise in the book, which is full of fascinating information, is that film was first shown in Worthing in 1896. That's ninety years before I showed up in the town with my crew to make my feature film *Wish You Were Here*. At the time, I was unaware that, as film-makers, we were part of an ongoing film-making tradition on that part of the south coast.

Incongruously, it all began along the south coast with a burst of activity at newly constructed film-studio space at Shoreham-by-Sea. By 1918, it had become the blue touchpaper for a cinematic explosion across the UK. Here were the trailblazers of early cinema, and this book offers extraordinary insights into their film-making on the south coast of England, a place that was to become known as Hollywood by the Sea.

During the silent film era, crowds would show up to watch the filming; it was a spectator sport. One of the biggest crowds turned out to watch a comic scene of two men trying to carry a piano through deep mud on a river bank – god knows how it got there. It was called *Moving a Piano*, of course. The rumour was that Charlie Chaplin had travelled from Hollywood to feature in the scene. On the day, the two actors were covered in so much mud the crowd couldn't tell if it was Chaplin or not. The rumour was never resolved. The sequence reminds me of a Laurel and Hardy film that both amused and alarmed me as a boy – they wreaked so much havoc – featuring Stan and Ollie delivering a piano up a flight of extremely high steps. You can find it on YouTube. Chaplin may not have appeared in Shoreham, but he did make a silent film called *Musical Tramp* in which – guess what? – he moves a piano up extremely high steps. Brilliant. Very funny. This leaves me wondering if Laurel and Hardy saw this film before they made theirs. And this is the wonderful thing about this book: it sends one off to looking for gems one might not ever have discovered.

Among the numerous stories of the films and filming at Hollywood by the Sea featured in the book, there is Joan Morgan. I must confess I had never heard of Joan.

A still from the *Wish You Were Here* shoot, with David Leland rehearsing with Emily Lloyd on Worthing seafront. 'I'm showing her how to pose like Betty Grable.' (Courtesy of Ian Pleeth)

She became a child star before the First World War, went to Hollywood when she was 15, returned and went on to star in numerous films made in Shoreham. Before the Second World War, she was linked to the Fascist movement, survived, made more films, and lived to be 99. One of her quotes strikes me as being particularly prescient for our times. Commenting on the British way of life, she said, 'We've been successful for so long that we still blindly believe in our ability to muddle through.'

Kevin Brownlow's piece on his encounters with Eric Sparks, a cantankerous and anti-social collector of transport films, is a knockout.

Discovering the Dome Cinema in Worthing when we were filming *Wish You Were Here* was a stroke of great good fortune. On the back row of the stalls, there were 'double' seats specially made for courting couples, with cupids in plaster relief on the wall behind them. I hope they're still there. At that time there were plans to demolish the Dome to make way for a high-rise car park. We did our bit to support the campaign to preserve the Dome. Good sense prevailed over commerce and the Dome survived. It is a cinematic treasure. Long may it remain.

Now read on ...

David Leland, 2017
Film director, screenwriter and actor

INTRODUCTION

Until recently a crumbling plaque fixed to the wall of the Pavilion Theatre at the land-end of Worthing Pier informed visitors that film was first shown in Worthing in 1896. One day during the summer of 2015 I was looking at this plaque when it struck me that the 120th anniversary of that event would be the perfect time for a project about the history of film in Sussex. I contacted the Heritage Lottery Fund with this suggestion, and was fortunate to secure the necessary funding for Worthing WOW to lead this project.

I had, as it happened, recently had a meeting with Ellen Cheshire, and I realised at once that she would be the perfect choice to be the project historian. And so began a year-long adventure across time, looking back at 120 years of film activity in Worthing and Shoreham. This culminated in a series of exhibitions and events in May and June 2016, a Heritage Trail app, and now this fascinating book, full of quirky facts, amusing anecdotes and insightful analysis.

There were a number of exciting discoveries along the way. Films thought to be lost were recovered, and new connections were established. Cinema-going, the history of cinema and film-making itself are interconnected worlds, and Ellen Cheshire and James Clarke have deftly interwoven them in the pages that follow.

The story begins at the time when music hall was the dominant form of popular entertainment, and the Electric Pictures no more than a novelty attraction. No one guessed that 'the Magic Lantern', as early cinema was also sometimes known, would within a few years become both a major art form and a massive industry generating billions of dollars of revenue. Cinema-going has survived the arrival of television and the DVD, and millions of people still attend regularly, watching everything from Hollywood blockbusters to obscure European films, children's adventures to cult classics.

Cheshire and Clarke take us on the twelve-decade journey from 1896 to 2016, stopping off to examine – among other things – silent films, early cinematographers, and Charlie Chaplin and Alfred Hitchcock's visits to Worthing. During that period cinemas have opened and cinemas have closed, but the art of film storytelling has remained as vibrant and innovative as ever.

Nearing the present day, this book looks at major films that were filmed in our area – including *The Da Vinci Code* – and notes the growing number of production companies that are active here, as well as the newly formed Sussex Film Office. These new bodies will help to ensure that the buildings and the landscape of Sussex continue to be immortalised on film.

Meanwhile, as a by-product of the Worthing WOW film project and the 2016 Festival, there is now a shiny new plaque on the side of the pier's southern pavilion, to remind future generations of the town's important place in the history of cinema.

Melody Bridges

Plaque marking the first 'film' screening in West Sussex at Southern Pavilion, unveiled in May 2016.

The Storytelling on Film Project: Then and Now – held in 2016 and funded by the Heritage Lottery Fund – consisted of two exhibitions, several school workshops and numerous special events, which were enjoyed by over 10,000 people. The discoveries and activities have been archived at a new webiste, www.filminsussex. co.uk, which, together with the present book, will ensure that the research of 2016 and the record of that year's festival will remain available to film historians and lovers of cinema.

Melody Bridges is the Artistic Director of Worthing WOW, a non-profit-making body that exists to promote arts, culture and heritage in Sussex. It provides a platform for new work, celebrates creativity, and encourages artistic expression.

PART 1

A NEW WAVE OF ENTERTAINMENT: FILM-MAKING IN WORTHING AND SHOREHAM

The history of British film-making is powerfully tied to the development of the medium. In early twentieth-century Worthing and Shoreham, pioneering film-makers set up their studios by the beach, making the most of the picturesque area as a place in which to put movies into motion. This section introduces key players and productions that emerged in the film-making history of the area, from sensitively rendered melodramas to thrifty 1950s B-movies.

1

MOVIES AND BUNGALOWS: THE STORY OF SHOREHAM BEACH

BY MARLIPINS MUSEUM, SUSSEX ARCHAEOLOGICAL SOCIETY

The early twentieth century saw a vibrant influx of new residents and industries to the small south coast seaside town of Shoreham. Of particular lasting importance was the establishment of 'bungalow town' and the development of the early film industry on Shoreham Beach for a decade from 1914–1924. The beach community thrived for many years until the sudden evacuation of residents and the clearing of the buildings at the outbreak of the Second World War.

Developing 'Bungalow Borough'

The spit of shingle beach that was to become known as Bungalow Town was largely undeveloped and uninhabited until the latter part of the nineteenth century.

The 1891 census for the area lists no residential beach properties other than the Shoreham Coast Guard Station and Shoreham Fort. However, the beginnings of the beach development are clearly there as the same census records three unoccupied 'beach huts'.

In 1879 a local oyster merchant, John Maple, had sited an old railway carriage on the beach to serve as a store for fishing equipment and as a part-time bathing hut. Maple later developed the building, and it became the bungalow 'Sea View'.

In 1896 there were just eleven dwellings listed on the beach. By 1900 there were 120 and in 1909 this had increased to 200 dwellings. The arrival of Marie Loftus, one of the country's most popular entertainers, is said to have led the theatrical colonisation of Bungalow Town. The idyllic setting soon attracted many of her friends from London – life on the beach offering a welcome respite to the pressures of appearing on stage. This 'bungalow boom' was also made possible with the advent of a direct train service from London in 1897.

Within just a few years the beach had become known as a popular bohemian holiday destination.

Building the Bungalows

Plots of land on the beach could be purchased through agents acting on behalf of the landowners. In 1900 the price of a plot was around £25 (now about £2,775). The plots were generally 20 sq. m and several people purchased double or even larger plots.

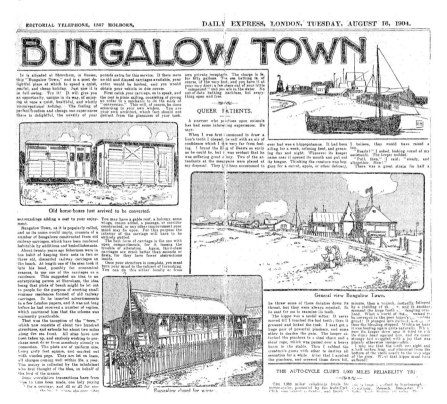

Feature in the *Daily Express* on the development of Bungalow Town, 16 August 1904.

The majority of owners had their holiday homes built around redundant railway carriages, which cost around £10 each (£1,100). Carriages, usually from the London, Brighton and South Coast Railway, once stripped of usable parts offered a comparatively quick and affordable means of building a holiday bungalow.

The bungalows were generally formed of two carriages placed, parallel to each other, on the simple foundation of a concrete 'raft' over the shingle. The space between the carriages would be swiftly and inexpensively roofed over with corrugated iron. The central space became one or two rooms and the coach compartments were converted into bedrooms and kitchens. Verandas were created at one or both ends and in several instances additional storeys were added.

There was no planning control and amongst the more typical bungalows were several that displayed an owner's individual taste – these included a castle, a Queen Anne-style mansion and a Chinese pagoda.

The beach was split into two areas: the east and west. A number of the bungalows along the eastern side, around what became Ferry Road, were considered 'shaky', with poorer foundations.

The proximity of the sea and the somewhat flimsy construction methods and materials meant that the bungalows were vulnerable to the elements. Fire and storm damage were a regular cause of loss; a newspaper article of 1935 reported that railway carriages were no longer to be allowed on the beach and all new properties had to be constructed of fire resistant materials.

Life on the Beach

Until the 1920s there was little development of infrastructure on the beach to support the bungalow colony.

Access to the beach remained difficult, especially on the eastern side. There were just a few rough roads and most people relied upon rowing boat ferries that operated from the town, though this service was weather dependent.

Built in 1910 the railway station Bungalow Halt served the western end of the beach until 1933. The first footbridge was constructed in 1921 but this was initially a toll bridge: 1d each way for adults, a halfpenny for children and 1d for bicycles.

Many of the bungalows were occupied by their owners but a considerable number were let as furnished rentals for long and short seasonal periods. The influx of visitors contributed significantly to the local economy.

One local in particular, butcher Tom Avis, took advantage of the affluent holidaymakers, declaring he 'made the wealthy blighters on the beach pay extra' (*Shoreham Herald*, 1914).

Sketch. July 30. 1913.

BATHING IN PYJAMAS: THE FREE AND EASY LIFE AT SHOREHAM.

A group of young people enjoying life at Shoreham in 1913 proved to be the envy of Londoners according to the *Daily Sketch*, 20 July 1913.

The End of an Era

Although the brief flourishing of the film-making companies came to an end in 1923, Bungalow Town continued to provide a haven for theatrical residents.

The carefree life the beach residents enjoyed came to an abrupt end in July 1940. As German forces amassed along the French coast the War Office demanded that all south-coast beaches should be made ready to defend the country in the event of an invasion.

Evacuation notices were issued to those living on the beach; residents were given just forty-eight hours to pack their possessions and vacate their homes.

The army was deployed to demolish the bungalows and the majority of the buildings were soon lost. The beach was then laid with a series of minefields and covered in barbed wire. Remarkably, a few of the beach homes escaped the destruction, and today visitors, if they look carefully enough, can find one or two of the original bungalows with a railway carriage at their heart.

Surprisingly, the glass daylight studio survived the Second World War but was eventually demolished in 1963.

BRIGHTON AND HOVE CINEMA PIONEERS

From the dawn of cinema there has been film-making on the south coast, and at the turn of the century the epicentre was Brighton and Hove. For more information on this important and vibrant moment in film-making history do visit the permanent exhibition at Hove Museum, or make use of the online resources on the Brighton Museums' website.

2

EARLY ACTUALITY FILMS: SUPERSTAR CINEMATOGRAPHER IN WORTHING

BY ELLEN CHESHIRE

In April 1898 one of the world's first superstar cameramen visited Worthing to capture the realities of a British seaside resort on film.

William Kennedy Dickson (1860–1935) was a Scottish inventor who moved to America in 1883 and worked with Thomas Edison. In 1889 Edison, keen to develop a machine that would 'do for the Eye what the phonograph does for the Ear', commissioned Dickson to make this a reality. Dickson and his team spent two years developing 'the Kinetoscope' and in 1891 unveiled their first working prototype; in 1892 he turned to producing films that would put the device into use. The following year saw the first public demonstration of the Kinetoscope. It may now be better known as a 'peep show' (or a 'what the butler saw') as this machine allowed only a single viewer to look through the small hole, and see a short roll of 35mm film on a continuous loop. On 14 April 1894 ten machines were installed at Kinetoscope Parlour in Broadway, New York, to great success. During that year Dickson made seventy-five films of approximately twenty seconds in length for these machines.

Unbeknown to Edison, Dickson was also secretly working with other inventors to create better and/or cheaper alternatives to the Kinetoscope. At Woodville Latham, with former Edison employee Eugene Lauste, they developed a system for showing much longer strips of film, and created an early projector, the Eidoloscope.

Some claim this combination of film and projector was the first commercial film screening in May 1895.

With Herman Casler he developed the much cheaper machine, 'the Mutoscape', which used a flipbook method of delivery (rather than film) and a large-format 70mm Biograph camera.

Dickson left Edison's in 1895 and with three other partners, including Casler, formed the American Mutoscope and Biograph Company. In 1897 he returned to Britain as manager and chief cameraman of British Mutoscope and Biograph Company. Using a Biograph camera he captured major events on film such as Queen Victoria's Diamond Jubilee procession (1897) as well as smaller local activities.

On 6 and 7 April 1898 he visited Worthing and over the two days he made at least seven films: three films of a Worthing lifeboat; two of the steamboat *Brighton Queen*; people walking along the seafront and a water polo match at West Worthing Baths. Three films are known to survive, two from the lifeboat sequence and the water polo match.

In its May 1898 edition, *The Optical Magic Lantern Journal* gave an account of Dickson's two days in Worthing:

On the 6th April the inhabitants of Worthing were suddenly startled by the report of a cannon, which meant to those 'not in the know', a ship in distress. Consequently crowds gathered quickly on the seafront, hastening westwards along the Marine Parade as far as the flagstaff opposite the coastguard station, where the lifeboat was ominously emerging from its shelter. Great excitement prevailed; four horses were connected, the crew donning their coats of cork and mounting with all the speed their pet-life saving apparatus – one of the many monuments of England's beneficence. Soon the command was given, 'Let her go!' On this occasion, however, that command had a double meaning, and many in the crowd were greatly puzzled as to the meaning of all they saw. Close to the esplanade stood a horse with a heavy cart behind it, laden with what connoisseurs call electric batteries, which send their mysterious powers through a red double cord up to a huge camera mounted on a rigid iron tripod, and inside of this instrument there was a reel holding a sensitised film about 200 feet long. This, too, was 'let go', to run its entire length down behind a lens, recording many impressions per second of the interesting procession rushing by towards the scene of action. As soon as the first performance was completed, the whole machinery was erected on the pier to take the launching and departure of the lifeboat. When this had been accomplished the mutograph [The Company's film camera], was loaded for the third time to photograph also the landing of the corky crew. For this event the spectators had to wait nearly two hours, during which time many of them had dispersed. As the boat was nearing the shore and surmounting the last few breakers, Mr Dickson shouted once more, 'Let her go!' When the lifeboat struck the beach many rushed forward to assist in pulling her up, while some of the crew jumped hastily out of the boat into the foaming waves, and quick as lightning, yet more carefully, laid upon the sand the body of a man drowned (?) for the purpose of pleasing sightseers and in the interest of science. Medical aid was, however, at hand, and by means of proper restoratives and a most scientific manipulation of breathing apparatus, the drowned mariner was soon able to return to his home and friends. And thus ended the noble work of the life-saving and animated photography. The sun was shining all the time, there was a good breeze blowing and plenty of sea – all very favourable circumstances, so that the pictures taken (about 4,000) ought to be very effective when finished and projected upon the screen. The following day the Worthing Swimming Club played some games of water polo, etc., in the big baths at West Worthing, while the mutograph was again actively looking on and taking it all in. (From *Optical Magic Lantern Journal*, Vol. 9 No. 108, May 1898 pp. 198–199)

These seven films were included in a half-hour compilation reflecting the contemporary world, first shown as part of three hours of music hall entertainment at the prestigious Palace Music Hall in London in December 1898.

On the outbreak of the Boer War in 1899, Dickson travelled to South Africa and spent several months filming the war. He wrote about his experiences in *The Biograph in Battle* published in 1901 (the first memoirs of a cameraman). He left British Biograph in 1903, which led to the end of his film career. For the remainder of his working life he was an electrical engineer.

3

SHOREHAM: ENGLAND'S HOLLYWOOD BY THE SEA

BY ELLEN CHESHIRE

In 1919 the Manchester-based film company Progress moved their film-making operation to Shoreham. In their company prospectus they highlighted the benefits of Shoreham as a location for film production:

> The climatic conditions of Shoreham-by-Sea are particularly suitable, and peculiarly adapted for daylight production. The air is wonderfully clear, and quite free from fogs, and as the studio is situated on a spot at least 50 miles from any real smoke, a pure and clean light may be obtained, probably unrivalled by any other place in England. Undoubtedly the Los Angeles of English production.

By this point the south coast had been attracting film-makers for over twenty years. Many of the British pioneers and experimenters of the electric pictures had been based in nearby Brighton and Hove.

Mavis Clare (centre) alongside Progress staff and stars on Shoreham Beach. (Courtesy of the Mavis Clare/Gillian Gregg Archive)

Brighton and County Film Company (1912)

W. Harold Speer founded the Brighton and County Film Company, and in May 1912 the company's only two films were released.

A plot description for *A Nurse's Devotion* (23 minutes) in Denis Gifford's *The British Film Catalogue* described the film as, 'Drama: Shoreham, Nurse adopts child she saves from sea and later inherits'. However, as no copies of the film have been found it is unclear whether it was actually shot in Shoreham. But it seems unlikely that a Brighton-based film company would set a film in Shoreham, if it wasn't actually filmed there.

His second film *The Motor Bandits* (17 minutes) has survived, and a copy is held by Screen Archive South East who summarise the film thus: 'An early professionally-made fiction film with intertitles which tells the story of a bank robbery and the subsequent hunt for the robbers. The film is notable for its use of a highly-developed narrative, generic conventions and location shooting.' The film was shot in Brighton and the South Downs and although difficult to pinpoint, it looks to be to the west of Shoreham where the coastline was less developed in 1912.

Sunny South Films (1914–15)

The first film company to base themselves at Shoreham was Sunny South Films. The British film magazine *The Bioscope* (1 October 1914) reported that they had:

> it on excellent authority that at an early date a new brand of British comedy subjects will be placed upon the market, and that a famous trio of leading comedians will be thereby concerned. The new company is the outcome of a partnership between Mr Will Evans of Drury Lane fame, and Mr F. L. Lyndhurst, a well-known scenic artist, and a studio is in the course of erection at a well-known seaside resort, where work is shortly to be commenced upon various originals productions. Included in the artistes who will appear in the these are, in addition to Mr Evans, Mr Arthur Conquest and Mr George Graves, who will give his sole services for films. There should, indeed, be a bright future for the 'comics', especially when one realises the undoubted drawing power of the names already mentioned and their well-advertised connection with one of the leading theatres in the world.

Both Lyndhurst and Evans had holiday homes in Shoreham and so knew the area well. The site they selected for their studio was at the then-abandoned Napoleonic Palmerston Fort at Shoreham. They filmed in the open air using the old parade ground as stage – the embankment shielded filming from curious onlookers. Here scenic painter Lyndhurst, with his assistant Geoffrey Dickinson, created backdrops (canvas stretched on wood frames) and simple sets, whilst his comic counterparts recreated some of their most popular music hall sketches and created new comic gems on film. The eight films made in 1914–15 by Sunny South were *Building a Chicken House*, *The Jockey*, *Will Evans' Comedies*, *Moving a Piano*, *The Showman's Dream*, *Tincture of Iron*, *Some Fun* and *A Study in Skarlit*.

Sunny South's most ambitious film was *The Showman's Dream* (1914) and was based on a sketch by Will Evans. Here, Evans plays the eponymous showman, Professor Evanso, who falls asleep and dreams that his circus is on fire and a tiger escapes. The film was shot at the Palmerston Fort against backdrops, with scenes of the showman in pursuit of his tiger (Arthur Conquest). It was filmed on location and included the Flood Arch, Brighton Road and Old Shoreham. In *West Sussex on the Silver Screen* there's a report that: 'During filming the tiger (Conquest) bumped into a member of the public coming out of the Red Lion pub and followed him up the Steyning Road. The scene was so funny that it was kept in.' The film also featured Nell Emerald and The Hon. Mrs Victor Bruce, who in the 1920s and '30s achieved international acclaim as a record-breaking racing motorist, speedboat racer and aviator.

DID CHARLIE CHAPLIN APPEAR IN *MOVING A PIANO*?

There have been several reports over the years that, 'In one comedy made at Shoreham Charlie Chaplin struggled in the river mud with a piano on a handcart, to the great amusement of locals who went along to watch.' (*Evening Argus*, 29 April 1970. Story repeated in *West Sussex Gazette*, 20 June 1996.) It looks like this rumour began in 1937 when Arthur Wilde was recalling Shoreham's early film-making days for the article 'Shoreham Was Once England's Hollywood' in *Sussex Daily News* (15 December 1937). He reports:

> Some residents can recall a film scene being 'shot' off the Dolphin Hard, near where the Footbridge now stands. Two comedians wheeled into the river mud a hand-truck, upon which was a piano and their slithering antics caused great amusement to the crowd. The film was called *Moving a Piano* and I have been told that one of the comedians was the great Charlie Chaplin. Sadly, this rumour is not true.

Following a successful stage career in British music hall with the Karno troupe, including extensive touring in America, in January 1914 Chaplin began his first gruelling year in Hollywood. In his first year working for Mack Sennett at Keystone Studios he made thirty-six films, leaving no time or inclination to make a three-week round trip back to England to push a piano in a muddy river in Shoreham!

Sealight (1915–16)

The following year Lyndhurst returned to Shoreham (without his previous three partners) and founded Sealight Films at King's Gap, a site adjacent to the Church of the Good Shepherd. The company was registered, according to *The Bioscope* (1 July 1915), on 15 June 1915 with a capital investment of £10,000 in £1 shares to 'carry on the business of manufacturers, hirers and renters of and dealers in cinematograph films, apparatus, posters and literature etc.' F.L. Lyndhurst of Lyndon, Shoreham-by-Sea, was listed as the sole managing director. Anyone interested in becoming a shareholder for this new venture were invited to apply to his solicitor, E.C. Webster of Lincoln's Inn. The minimum investment was for 100 shares. Adjusted for inflation, £10,000 would now be worth just over £1 million; £100 = £10,408.20.

A glass daylight studio. (Courtesy of John Payne)

Progress Film Company filming at the glasshouse studio, Shoreham. (Courtesy of the Mavis Clare/ Gillian Gregg Archive)

With his loan of £10,000 Lyndhurst commissioned a glasshouse studio, using special glass that magnified the natural light (75ft by 45ft, with a height of 30ft), erected on a thick concrete base on the shingle from a south London firm who specialised in greenhouses. Here, according to the BFI film database, he directed only one short feature film, the drama *A Man and a Woman* (1916).

Filming became increasingly difficult with the war raging across the Channel, and it is believed that a combination of personal circumstances and financial pressures led to Lyndhurst defaulting on his mortgage and subsequently selling the studio to Olympic Kine Trading Company. Olympic were film renters with offices in Upper St Martin's Lane in London. There is no evidence of any filming at Shoreham again until the Manchester-based Progress Film Company set up there in summer 1919.

Progress Film Company (1919–22)

Frank E. Spring worked as an accountant before joining his brother as co-owner of a newspaper in St Annes-on-Sea in Lancashire. Through this he became interested in the film business and began screening films in a public hall in St Annes, from 1912. With Fred Rigg (as company secretary) he founded Progress in 1918 and made several films including *Democracy* (1918) prior to relocating production to Shoreham.

The crowd in the concert hut at Smith's bungalow, along with Progress staff and stars. (Courtesy of the Mavis Clare/Gillian Gregg Archive)

Their first season at Shoreham was in 1919. Spring, acting as producer, brought in Sidney Morgan (who had been writing and directing films since 1914) as screenwriter/director and Stanley Mumford as cinematographer. Morgan in turn hired his daughter, Joan, who took the lead in eight films, whilst a little later Spring's daughter, Mavis Clare (whose real name was Kathleen Spring), took on smaller roles before graduating to star parts when Joan left Progress to work for other film producers. The family atmosphere continued, with Mumford bringing his brother Arthur on board to work in the studio's lab. With agent John Payne taking on the role of casting, Progress built around them a repertory company of actors who lived and worked together. Some actors, such as Nell Emerald, had been established on the south coast for some time, whilst others stayed for the summer shooting period in Studio Rest, a twenty-bedroom property, and The Galleon, which provided sleeping and living accommodation for cast and crew.

Progress bought the studio in 1920 for £3,500 and over the years they developed the site further by adding a yard for building sets and storage for set, props equipment etc. Later an editing suite, preview theatre and a small laboratory for processing film were added. Prior to this, film was sent to London to be processed, and the nearby Bijou Cinema was used for screening rushes. In his memoirs Mumford wrote that, 'This Studio was the only one in the country where artists and key staff lived on the job. They had the time of their lives at this seaside studio.'

It is believed that by 1918 there were thirty-three film studios in the UK, with Shoreham's glasshouse being the only remaining studio that did not have artificial light (Low, 1971:250). Shoreham was acclaimed for its clear skies and long hours of sunshine and was therefore ideal when full light was needed, but it was harder to create mood lighting. For this, Mumford employed diffusers and reflectors made by

Cast and crew on their way to film *The Mayor of Casterbridge* on location. (Courtesy of the Mavis Clare/Gillian Gregg Archive)

Filming of *The Mayor of Casterbridge* in Steyning. (Courtesy of the Mavis Clare/Gillian Gregg Archive)

pasting silver paper onto plywood and angled onto actors for creative lighting. The weather did cause problems, as the glasshouse studio had no ventilation whatsoever; extreme heat would make the studio unbearable and actors' make-up would run. Clouds moving overhead could ruin a shot, so an assistant was employed to warn of any impending light changes. According to Mumford's memoirs: 'It was quite good fun working in the studio almost in bathing dress on hot days – on many occasions while a new set was being erected, all those not concerned would walk out of the studio down to the beach in the sea and have a cooling bathe.' At night, once the cameras had stopped turning, Joan Morgan recalled, 'We used to play roulette with newly-minted farthings from the bank and all the music hall people would come. Or we would be popping into each other's bungalows to eat or for coffee. It was truly idyllic.' (*Daily Mail*, 6 June 1996)

The company schedule was to spend the summer season (usually April to September) filming at Shoreham and the winter months reading and planning the next summer's output.

In its four years at Shoreham, Progress made seventeen movies, filming in the glasshouse studio as well as on location. Joan Morgan recalled driving around Sussex on Sundays looking at potential houses they could use. Filming also took place further afield, for instance they travelled to Scotland for *The Lilac Sunbonnet* (1922) where they filmed at Trossachs near Loch Lomond, for *By Berwyn Banks* (1920) they went to North Wales, and for *Two Little Wooden Shoes* (1920) and *Rogues of the Turf* (1923) they travelled to Belgium and France, filming in Brussels and Paris amongst other locations.

The Mayor of Casterbridge (1922) was Morgan's last film for Progress. It was made whilst Joan was filming on location in South Africa in a film version of Rider Haggard's *Swallows*. Frank E. Spring's daughter Kathleen took on the lead role of Elizabeth, changing her name to Mavis Clare. It was filmed partly in Dorset and made with the full endorsement of Thomas Hardy who visited location filming at Dorchester. He described Mavis as 'my Elizabeth'.

Morgan directed fifteen films between 1919 and 1922, but he and Joan left midway through the fourth season and Wilfred Noy came over from America especially to take up the directing mantle for what were to be Progress's last two Shoreham films: *Rogues of the Turf* (1923) and *Little Miss Nobody* (1923). These last two films are occasionally listed as being produced by Carlton Film Company, but this was a name given to the production arm of Progress, not a different organisation. The fire at the studio in December 1922 saw the end of Progress's time at Shoreham, and final scenes for *Little Miss Nobody* where shot at Twickenham.

Although Progress were to make no further films, the company wasn't wound-up until 1929 when the Shoreham studio site was sold back to its original owners.

Sidney Morgan and Frank Spring continued to work together – making films for Astra-National Production. Sidney can also be seen on screen in Alfred Hitchcock's *Juno and the Paycock* (1930) as Joxer Daly. He was secretary of the British Association of Directors in 1931. Throughout his career he directed forty-seven films and was instrumental in the founding of the 1927 Cinematograph Films Act, which ushered in a wave of low-budget British films, known as 'quota quickies'.

Frank E. Spring owned a small cinema circuit, which included the Theatre Royal, Oldham, and the Hippodrome in St Helens. According to his granddaughter Gillian Gregg, 'He liked the good life, and lived the good life!' (*Silver Screen, Silent Voices*. Cinemedia, 2008)

BUNGALOW TOWN ABLAZE
BY ELLEN CHESHIRE AND STANLEY MUMFORD

Stanley Mumford (1888–1977) was Progress's cinematographer at Shoreham from 1919 to 1922. He began his film career in 1901 when he left school aged 14 to join a firm of scenic artists who were painting backdrops for sideshows. Aged 18 he went on tour with a show to maintain the sets and, as he had an interest in photography, run the Bioscope.

When he spotted an advertisement in *The Stage* for a scenic artist with an interest in cinematography and photography for Williamson & Co. film company in Hove he applied and in 1907 he joined the team with pay of 30 shillings a week. The first film he worked on was *The Rent Collector* (1908). The following year he joined the Warwick Trading Co. at Ealing Studios as a cameraman. Warwick was taken over by Will Barker and became The Barker Motion Picture Company. It was whilst working for Barkers filming for Pathé News that Mumford would capture a moment on film that has become part of political and social history.

On 4 June 1913 Mumford took up a prime camera position at Tattenham Corner on the day of the derby at Epsom racecourse, as he wrote in his memoirs:

There was that feeling that something was in the air, because so many police were on duty... I remember the hushed silence that seemed everywhere. With my eyes focused to the small viewfinder on the camera I waited until I could just see a small blink of horse and then I started to crank the camera. All of a sudden from under the rails opposite me a woman dashed out and ran bang slap into the middle of those thundering horses ... before you could gasp she was knocked flying and rolled over ... the horse and jockey coming down with her.

Stanley Mumford had caught on film suffragette Emily Davison's attempt to disrupt the race by pinning a sash to the King's horse. When writing his memoirs in the early 1950s he still recalled 'the impact of that horse on the woman I shall never forget, she just bounced like a rubber ball'.

In 1914 Mumford reported for military service and initially his entrance was deferred as he was working on important propaganda films for the war effort, but in January 1915 he joined the Norfolk Yeomanry. After the war he returned to film-making, first at the Garrick Film Company in Surbiton and then he signed a contract with Sidney Morgan to join Progress at Shoreham as their cinematographer. His brother, Arthur, joined him, taking charge of the lab. They lived with other cast and crew at Studio Rest, but unlike the rest of them who left at the end of the summer season, the Mumford brothers stayed on at Shoreham throughout the winter season to keep up an eye on the properties and to finish up any outstanding post-production work.

This was most fortunate on the 'bitter cold night' in December 1922, when a major fire broke out. As Mumford recalled in his memoirs:

It must have been about 12.30 ... I heard a terrific crash. I jumped up opening my eyes, then I got the biggest fright of my life – a large sheet of flame was coming from the opposite bungalow direct at our bungalow[,] licking the glass windows until they crashed in.

A sheet of flame came towards me[.] I shouted at my brother and rushed towards him and he was doing the same. We both met in our dining room, both in night attire.

Our bungalow was well alight and the one opposite just a blazing furnace.

After recovering from our first shock my brother rushed back to his bedroom to rescue his personal belongings and threw them out on the beach, then remembering suddenly the season's negatives which were under my bed. Shouting to him to give me a hand we managed to drag the heavy tin trunk out of the bungalow and down the beach into the studio for safety.

By the time we returned the whole show was well alight. Then I suddenly remembered the camera apparatus so we both made a dive for this and automatically I started to put up the tripod, my brother handing me up the camera saying 'What are you going to do?' I was too scared to reply[,] thinking what a daft thing to do, load a camera in a burning building, I saw we might as well take a picture of the old place before it leaves us.

We got outside with the camera, the wind nearly taking us off our feet. It was blowing a proper gale, the whole bungalow opposite us and several large bungalows adjoining, apart from our own were well alight. The tragedy was [,] owing to the Norfolk Bridge being closed, the fire brigade from Shoreham could not reach the area so it was many hours before Worthing fire brigade arrived. We stood spellbound at the sight that met us, the night was lit up for miles around.

My brother made a rush towards one of the bungalows because he thought he heard a cry for help. We managed to pull out from a downstairs room an old lady who was bed-ridden and passed her to [the] care of others now milling around, then I moved toward another with the camera and took quite a few shots.

Entering a bungalow I thought my brother was in, I took a quick look around and set the camera up and started to shoot. The whole room was ablaze and I was getting some remarkable shots when all of a sudden with a cracking noise the roof over my head collapsed, knocking both me and the camera flat. Picking myself up I found my pyjamas were burning. Quickly beating out the flames I rescued the camera which was not damaged, thank goodness, but almost red hot. I managed to crawl out but not the way I went in, but through a hole burnt in the wall.

I found myself outside near the sea, my brother rushed up to me and called my attention to stacks of furniture and peoples' belongings that had been dragged from the bungalows all along the beach, from the bungalows that were burning and from others that the high wind was blowing the flames towards, they being built so close together that one burning caught the other.

But what my brother was drawing my attention to was the tide that had risen quickly with the gale and was washing the furniture [out] to sea. I took several shots of these people in night attire trying to rescue their belongings, in many cases the furniture was seen drifting out to sea.

It all seemed to be the irony of fate, saving this furniture from the fire and then having it destroyed by sea.

Automatically I found myself in another house. I was so hot I had to pivot my face from the heat. The staircase was a mass of flames, a cat shot past the camera panic stricken. Great pieces of blazing material kept dropping on the camera and myself, then an extra burst of flame on the staircases crashed and caught me full on the face – I retreated[,] dragging the camera after me outside. I just passed out! When I came to I was lying on the beach shivering with cold.

Well, there was no sleep that night. At daylight I took several shots of the wreckage, showing scenery the 'morning after the night before' then we went to see what we could do to salvage our personal belongings which were strewn about the beach. However, we did very well after our adventure. I got in touch with Pathé Gazette early in the morning, and put the negative on the train. It was a news scoop for them and [a] fat cheque for us.

Following the fire, Mumford finished working on *Little Miss Nobody* at the far more up-to-date Twickenham Studios. He made two further films with Sidney Morgan. In 1927 he returned to newsreel films and joined British Pictorial Productions. For them he filmed the funeral of George V in 1936 and the coronation and crowning of the king and queen on 12 May 1937. During the Second World War he became a war correspondent. His last major assignment was in August 1948 when he flew to Amsterdam to film the first assembly of the World's Council of Churches and the coronation of Princess Juliana of Holland. British Pictorial was bought out by Rank in 1949, and Mumford retired, receiving a small pension for life. Looking back at his forty-two-year career in film he wrote: 'I feel I am one of the pioneers, that I laid the carpet down in the film industry, for others to walk over. The only thing in those early days was, we liked our job and took an interest in it. Everybody was in it for art sake, not for what they got out of it.'

You can watch Mumford's footage from this night in the Pathé Newsreel released in late December 1922 on the Pathé News website – search for 'Bungalow Town Ablaze'.

Quotes from 'Forty Years Behind a Movie Camera – Interesting Highlights of my Experiences in the Industry' by Stanley (Percy) Mumford held at BFI National Archive.

Walter West Productions (1922–23)

Walter West (1885–1958) had made over fifty films and produced a further thirty under his production company Broadwest, many of them starring the Australian actress Valerie Hobson. This company folded in September 1921, at which point he founded Walter West Productions and it was under this name that he filmed at Shoreham in 1922–23. The two films shot during this period were *Hornet's Nest* and *Was She Justified?*, starring American actress Florence Turner, who had achieved international fame as 'the Vitagraph Girl'.

Further scenes for *Hornet's Nest* were filmed in Washington, near Storrington, with local people featured as extras. *Hornet's Nest* was based on a novel by Andrew Soutar, and centres around the village blacksmith's pregnant daughter who kills herself when the squire's son rejects her. A 6,102ft version was released in 1924, and a shorter two-reeler version was released in 1926. Joining Turner in the cast were Fred Worth, James Knight, Lewis Gilbert, Kathleen Vaughan, Cecil Morton York, Nora Swinburne, Jeff Barlow and Arthur Walcott. *Was She Justified?* was based on the play *The Pruning Knife* by Maud Williamson and Andrew Soutar, in which a jealous man's wife fakes her death and drives him mad by pretending his daughter is illegitimate. The cast featured Florence Turner, Lewis Gilbert, Ivy Close, John Reid, George Bellamy and Arthur Walcott.

With these two films completed, the studios and associated building were left abandoned. In 1929 Progress sold the site back to Mr Easter, from whom Lyndhurst had bought the property from in 1915. And so Shoreham's dreams of becoming Britain's answer to Hollywood came to an end.

Bungalow Town remained a popular retreat of theatre and film folk in need of a few days' rest (and play) between engagements until the outbreak of the Second World War.

How could anyone have known that a jolly young lad, who holidayed at Shoreham in the mid 1920s with film director Graham Cutts, would go on to be one of the world's most famous directors. Photographs recently came to light of Alfred Hitchcock frolicking in Shoreham with his future wife Alma Reveille amongst others. If you pop 'Alfred Hitchcock' and 'Shoreham' into a search engine you'll find them.

4

PROGRESS FILMS AT SHOREHAM

BY ELLEN CHESHIRE

Sweet and Twenty (filmed 1919, released 1920)
From the play by Basil Hood
Director: Sidney Morgan
Cast: Langhorne Burton, Arthur Lennard, Marguerite Blanche, George Keene, George Bellamy, Nell Emerald
After being court-martialled, a cleric's son tries to redeem himself in Australia.

The Scarlet Wooing (filmed 1919, released 1920)
Original screenplay by Sidney Morgan
Director: Sidney Morgan
Cast: Joan Morgan, Marguerite Blanche, Eve Balfour, George Bellamy, George Keene, Arthur Walcott
'It was about an author's sensational novel paying for his daughter's operation but also leading his sister-in-law astray.' Joan Morgan in *Classic Images* No. 178, April 1990.

Lady Noggs (filmed 1919, released 1920)
From the children's stories by Edgar Jepsen, a story in *Windsor Magazine* and play by Cicely Hamilton
Director: Sidney Morgan
Cast: Joan Morgan, George Keene, George Bellamy, Yolande Duquette, James Prior
Sussex locations: Castle Goring and St Mary's Bramber

Taking a break during filming of *The Scarlet Wooing* (aka *The Wooing of April*). (Courtesy of the Mavis Clare/Gillian Gregg Archive)

'... was about an adopted orphan saving a Member of Parliament's grandson from foreign travels and Lady Noggs was the dogooder who really would pull the strings.' Joan Morgan in *Classic Images* No. 178, April 1990.

The Black Sheep (filmed 1919, released 1920)
From the serial by Ruby M. Ayres in the *Daily Mirror*
Director: Sidney Morgan
Cast: Marguerite Blanche, Eve Balfour, George Bellamy, George Keene, Arthur Lennard
'... proved to be a great success ... Thoroughly artistic from every viewpoint, the film contains many scenes of rural beauty whilst the wonderfully lighted concluding picture drew hearty applause from the audience. The plot is plentifully sprinkled with dramatic moments and is splendidly photographed. George Keene and Marguerite Blanche being an ideal pair of lovers, with Eve Balfour and Arthur Lennard respectively the "heavy woman" and the comic relief. Sidney Morgan is deserving of praise.' *The Era*, 17 March 1920.

Little Dorrit (filmed in 1920, released 1920)
From the novel by Charles Dickens
Director: Sidney Morgan
Cast: Lady Tree, Joan Morgan, Langhorne Burton, Compton Coutts, J. Denton-Thompson, George Foley, George Bellamy, Arthur Walcott, Judd Green, Betty Doyle, Mary Lyle
Sussex locations: Nyman's Gardens, Handcross.
Elsewhere: George Inn, Southwark
'Sidney Morgan is to be heartily congratulated on his adaptation and production of *Little Dorrit* shown to a large and enthusiastic audience ... The characters are particularly well chosen and acted. Miss Joan Morgan plays Amy Dorrit with a simplicity and naturalness that it would be difficult to improve upon. Lady Tree gives a fine dramatic performance of Mrs Clenman and Langhorne Burton is equally successful as Arthur Clenman ... The photography is excellent with some fine tinted effects being artistically introduced ... a most satisfactory British production.' *The Era*, 1 September 1920.

Two Little Wooden Shoes (filmed in 1920, released 1920)
From the novel by Ouida
Director: Sidney Morgan
Cast: Joan Morgan, Langhorne Burton, J. Denton-Thompson, Constance Backner, Maud Cressall, Faith Bevan, Ronald Power
Location: Brussels and Paris
'About a sick Parisian artist in Brussels and a flower-girl who fall in love. When he has gone back to Paris she goes on foot to join him there, wearing out her little wooden shoes or 'sabots' on the way. When she finds him, he is carousing with a model and other gorgeous women. She is so upset that she drowns herself.' Joan Morgan in *Classic Images* No. 178, April 1990.

The Woman of the Iron Bracelets (filmed in 1920, released 1921)
From the novel by Frank Barrett
Director: Sidney Morgan
Cast: Eve Balfour, Arthur Walcott, Alice de Winton, George Bellamy, George Keene, Marguerite Blanche
A woman fleeing from a murder charge helps a disowned heir prove his stepfather is a criminal hypnotist.

The Children of Gibeon (filmed in 1920, released 1920)
From the novel by Sir Walter Besant
Director: Sidney Morgan

Cast: Joan Morgan, Langhorne Burton, Arthur Lennard, Eileen McGrath, Sydney Fairbrother, Alice de Winton, Charles Cullum, Barbara MacFarlane
Lady Eldridge adopts the daughter of a criminal and raises her alongside her own children.

By Berwyn Banks (filmed in 1920, released in 1920)
From the novel by Allen Raine
Director: Sidney Morgan
Cast: Langhorne Burton, Arthur Lennard, Eileen McGrath, Judd Green
Location: North Wales
The amnesiac son of an Anglican vicar marries the daughter of a dissenter.

A Man's Shadow (filmed in 1920, released in 1920)
From the play by Robert Buchanan from the French
Director: Sidney Morgan
Cast: Langhorne Burton, Arthur Lennard, J. Denton-Thompson, Violet Graham, Warris Linden, Gladys Mason, Sidney Paxton, Babs Ronald
A man murders a usurer and is betrayed by his ex-wife.

Moth and Rust (filmed in 1921, released in 1921)
From a story by Mary Cholmondeley
Director: Sidney Morgan
Cast: Sybil Thorndike, Langhorne Burton, Malvina Longfellow, George Bellamy, Ellen Nicholls, Cyril Raymond, Malcolm Tod
A girl burns her brother's letters to a usurer's dead wife and is accused of burning his IOUs.

The Mayor of Casterbridge (filmed in 1921, released in 1921)
From the novel by Thomas Hardy
Director: Sidney Morgan
Cast: Fred Groves, Mavis Clair, Pauline Peters, Warwick Ward, Nell Emerald
Sussex Locations: The old White Horse Hotel in Steyning High Street was used as the Mayor's house
Other Locations: Dorchester, Dorset
Of his dealings with Progress, scholar T.R. Wright, in his book *Thomas Hardy on Screen*, notes that 'On February 1921, Hardy was wondering whether to insert the words "No alteration or adaptation being such as to burlesque or otherwise misrepresent the general character of the novel" into the agreement with the Progress Film Company' (p. 52). Wright also notes that Hardy suggested that Morgan refer to a photographic guidebook entitled *Thomas Hardy's Wessex* (1913) 'for guidance'.

A Lowland Cinderella (filmed in 1921, released 1921) aka *A Highland Maid*
From the novel by S.R. Crockett
Director: Sidney Morgan
Cast: Joan Morgan, Nell Emerald, Mary Carnegie, Mavis Clare, George Foley, Ralph
    Forbes, Eileen Grace, Kate Philips, Charles Levy, Cecil Susands, Frances Wetherall
Sussex locations: The Hotel Metropole, Brighton
'I played the girl, Hester Stirling, who starts as the poor relation, and then goes to
    the ball in feathers and pearls. George Foley was my uncle who steals rubies and
    then makes false accusations.' Joan Morgan in *Classic Images* No. 178, April 1990.

The Lilac Sunbonnet (filmed in 1922, released 1922)
From a story by S.R. Crockett
Director: Sidney Morgan
Cast: Joan Morgan, Arthur Lennard, Warwick Ward, Nell Emerald, Lewis Dayton,
    Forrester Harvey, Charles Levy, Pauline Peters, A. Harding Steerman
Location: Trossachs, near Loch Lomond
'The charming [film] has its setting in the beautiful Highland scenery. The hero
    is young Ralph Peden, a student of divinity qualifying for the ministry, and the
    heroine a pretty girl named Winsome, who imagines she is the daughter of the
    elderly couple with whom she lives, but who later is made acquainted with the
    fact that she is the daughter of a man who has run away and married at Gretna
    Green his friend's betrothed sweetheart, her father being none other than the
    minister of the local kirk. The acting is good all round, Miss Joan Morgan as
    the heroine and Warwick Ward as the hero being particularly well suited. The
    magnificent Highland scenery and some finely tinted moonlight scenes are an
    attractive feature of this excellent production. 9 ½.' *The Era*, 19 July 1922.

Fires of Innocence (filmed in 1922, released 1923)
From the novel *A Little World Apart* by George Stevenson
Director: Sidney Morgan
Cast: Joan Morgan, Arthur Lennard, Bobbie Andrews, Nell Emerald, Marie Illington,
    Madge Tree
Sussex Locations: Bramber Village and the Church of the Good Shepherd, Shoreham
Elsewhere: Either Poole or Torquay
'It was about a village vicar's son stealing a brooch and blaming his sister. Bobbie
    Andrews, another child-star, was in it ... we were doing a love-scene in a sort of
    rose-garden, and Bobbie wouldn't look down. He said: "I don't feel a bit in the
    mood to see you!"' Joan Morgan in *Classic Images* No. 178, April 1990.

Rogues of the Turf (filmed in 1922, released 1923)
From the play by John F. Preston
Director: William Noy
Cast: Mavis Clare, Fred Groves, Olive Sloane, Dora Lennox, James Lindsay, Robert Vallis, James Readen
Sussex Locations: New Salts Farm and Ferry Road, Shoreham
Other Locations: Lingfield Racing Stables in Surrey, Belgium and France
'A racing melodrama with all the classic elements of dubious characters switching of the favourite and even doping before the big race. The favourite gets cut adrift on a barge at sea!' *West Sussex on the Silver Screen*.

Filming on location recalled by Arthur Wilde in *Sussex Daily News* (15 December 1937):

> I remember seeing a large crowd of spectators who gathered in a meadow near New Salts Farm one lovely July evening in 1922 to see part of this film being made. A large marquee had been erected for taking scenes of the Turf Ball and it was really fascinating to watch the shadows of the dancers and the company flitting about the brilliantly illuminated interior, and to hear the music of the orchestra. In connection with this film the exciting capture of a runaway racehorse can be recalled on the sands off Ferry Road.

Little Miss Nobody (filmed in 1922, released 1923)
From the play by H. Graham
Director: William Noy
Cast: Flora le Breton, Aubrey Fitzgerald, Ben Field, Sydney Paxton, Donald Searle, Gladys Jennings, John Stuart, Eva Westlake, James Reardon
The caretaker of a Scottish castle tries to trick his aunt into believing that some of the guests are aristocrats.

The dates quoted are taken from *Cinema West Sussex: The First Hundred Years* (filmed dates) and the BFI website (release date). Where original reviews or quotes about the film were not found, the plot summary is from the BFI website.

5

A CLOSE LOOK AT
A LOWLAND CINDERELLA

BY JAMES CLARKE

A Lowland Cinderella (1921)
Directed by Sidney Morgan
Cinematography by Stanley Mumford
Screenplay by Sidney Morgan
From a novel by S.R. Crockett

Nell Emerald – Megsy
Joan Morgan – Hester Stirling
George Foley – David Stirling
Ralph Forbes – Master of Darrock
Eileen Grace – Claudia Torpichan
Kate Philips – Grandmother Stirling
Charles Levey – Dr Silvanus Torpichan
Cecil Susands – Tom Torpichan
Frances Wetherall – Duchess of Niddisdale
Mavis Clare – Ethel Torpichan

There was a magic moment, sustained over several years, when the Progress Film Company enjoyed the fruits of a commercially viable film production base at their studio in Shoreham-by-Sea. Perhaps their best-regarded movie was their adaptation of *Little Dorrit*. However, several other titles also proved real accomplishments and one of these was *A Lowland Cinderella*. As its charmingly illustrated opening intertitle informs us this is, 'An original story by Allyn B. Carrick, suggested by the favourite fairy tale, *CINDERELLA*.'

A Lowland Cinderella. Front right are Joan Morgan and Ralph Forbes, while behind to the left are Mavis Clare and an unknown actor.

A Lowland Cinderella. From left to right are Joan Morgan, Frances Wetherall, Mavis Clare and Eileen Grace. (Courtesy of the Mavis Clare/Gillian Gregg Archive)

Dismissing any of the fairy tale's overtly fantastical elements, *A Lowland Cinderella*, like its inspiring source material, is a story about class divisions and about how a generous heart wins out over a grasping and selfish one.

The story is set in Scotland and London but all of the location filming, as the sharp-eyed viewer will readily see, has clearly been achieved amidst the gentle undulations of the chalk-earthed South Downs, just north of Shoreham. So, too, the cottage exterior where a fair bit of the story plays out is characteristic of the Sussex rustic style. The film's appealing use of location was not lost on reviewers when the film was first released.

In *The Film Renter & Moving Picture News* (24 December 1921), the reviewer comments that: 'The setting of this story is most effective, and some of the lowland scenes are extremely well done, while the ball given by the Duchess of Niddersdale is a veritable triumph of screen-craft on its elaboration of detail.'

The story of *A Lowland Cinderella* centres around young Hester (the Cinderella-inspired heroine of the story) who becomes embroiled with a family who endeavour to deprive her of what is rightfully hers: the jewels mined by her father in Burma. Without wanting to give away the story's denouement, it won't surprise you to know that the forces of goodness and honesty rightly prevail.

The film's performances are, perhaps, surprisingly effective. Nell Emerald as Megsy, Hester's caring 'nurse' at the cottage in Scotland, ably communicates her warm-hearted and empathetic sense and protective way towards Hester. Several times, Megsy embraces the slightly built Hester (Joan Morgan).

The plot device of the rubies and their journey through the story are satisfyingly resolved and the storytelling convention of setting story elements up early on in order to pay them off much later on works excellently – notably in relation to Hester's expectation about how her father would one day arrive back home from his travels.

The performances in the film suggest how actors of the time were beginning to understand the degree to which the inner life of characters could be expressed with relatively little gesture and facial expression. There is a scene when Dr Torpsichan looks at the bag of rubies on his desk and deviously ponders the situation at hand. It's a nicely understated moment that contrasts with the return of Hester's father into the story at Dr Torpsichan's London home where his 'heroic' and unexpected return is given due flourish.

Let's quote again from the big thumbs-up review that *The Film Renter & Moving Picture News* (24 December 1921) gave. Here's the reviewer commenting on the performances in the film:

> For the success that this production is likely to achieve it will have to thank youthful Joan Morgan to a considerable extent. Here is a really gifted young actress who has talent as well as looks to commend her, and who is likely to go

very far indeed in her profession as she gains in age and experience. She makes a most charming figure as the 'Cinderella' who gives her name to the story, and makes instant appeal to all hearts so soon as she first appears. She has that gift of winsomeness that is but rarely seen on the screen, and is quite ideal for this part … a distinct triumph for Joan Morgan, and we heartily congratulate her upon it.

With its picturesque exterior location framing of actors against the landscape, the film's interior set action is more stage-like, and understandably so. Some of the film's interior material was shot at the Metropole Hotel in Brighton.

This film was produced at a time when the language of telling a story in cinematic terms (the early stages of what would constitute the grammar of cinema) was still being explored and conventions were settling into place. All of that said, *A Lowland Cinderella* displays a number of by-then established conventions of how best to frame actors in order to see their facial expressions and read their body language and gestures, and the cuts from close-ups and mid-shots to wider shots have an ease to them that makes for a pretty transparent kind of storytelling, allowing the viewer to focus their energies on empathising with the characters. There is a beautiful shot late in the film's third act when we see Hester leaning against a plough with the rising land in the background behind her.

The film is well structured and the main plot and the several subplots are all threaded together very satisfyingly over the course of just one hour of screen time. Enhancing it all is Richard Durrant's witty, modern score (commissioned by Screen Archive South East) that, in relation to the early sequences particularly, revels in a plaintive air.

Thought lost, this treasure of British film history was rediscovered in America in the 1990s under the title *A Highland Maid*.

6

SCORING A LOWLAND CINDERELLA

BY RICHARD DURRANT

Once upon a time I was commissioned to compose a score for a live performance and screening of *A Lowland Cinderella*. This special event was at Lancing College in the presence of the star of the film Joan Morgan in June 1996 as part of the *100 Years of Cinema* commemorations. Funding had been raised to restore this 'lost' film by Adur Arts development officer Louise Brattle and Screen Archive South East director Frank Gray, with additional help from the Arts Council.

Looking back to the time of the commission my strongest memory is of family loss and sadness. A few months before the premiere, my older brother, Eddie, lost his short battle with cancer and during his illness our father, Harry, was diagnosed with a brain tumour. I was also working on a score for BBC television's Easter commission, and the final day to submit the recording was the day of my brother's funeral. With *Cinderella* falling behind schedule I had to force myself back into the studio, however, it wasn't long before this strange little film became a wonderful distraction and writing for a live performance became a real pleasure.

In 1996 the business end of my studio was an eight-track tape recorder, a rudimentary Apple computer and a VHS player. There was also a clever little box that was able to synchronise all three, allowing me to produce music for TV and film, running the VHS tape backwards and forwards. Because *Cinderella* was for live performance I made a decision (with hindsight perhaps not my wisest) to use a combination of headphone cues, triggered by a machine code printed onto the video and midi sounds to act as audio cues for the musicians. I typed up the score using the back end of a programme called Cubase that could just about generate staffs and notes, and I recorded the midi/audio cues using a Korg M1 keyboard.

ELECTRIC PICTURES

Every project comes with a budget and *Cinderella* afforded me a quartet. I chose a cello for its large musical and expressive range, double bass for its cultural baggage and weight, percussion because I needed the kitchen sink and myself to play and direct at the same time. Most composers write with particular individuals in mind. I booked cellist Dave Burrowes (Royal Philharmonic, BBC), Tony Hougham (Royal Opera House) and Tom Arnold, a great, versatile musician and fellow harmonium lover.

The premiere was truly splendid, and a year later we resurrected the performance at the Church of the Good Shepherd. Here we recorded the live performance of the music which can be heard today on the only available version of the film. As in the shows, we played to the film and the musicians followed both the action and my directions from where I sat with my guitar, mandolin, banjo, cello and harmonium.

As with all good fairy tales, there is a happy ending. Louise, Adur Arts development officer, and I got married and we've lived happily in Shoreham with our children ever since.

7

'LOST' PROGRESS FILM FOUND: *FIRES OF INNOCENCE*

BY ELLEN CHESHIRE

Popular local history of the films shot at Shoreham Fort and Shoreham Beach from 1914 to 1923 has it that only one film survived in full, *A Lowland Cinderella* (1921) and two in part *Little Dorrit* (1920) and *The Mayor of Casterbridge* (1921). As part of this HLF-funded project for Worthing WOW film historian Ellen Cheshire, with help from Tony Fletcher, rediscovered this Progress film, previously thought lost. The images are from the pair's viewing at the BFI on a Steenbeck film-viewing table. This is the first time such extensive images from the film have been seen since the film's release in 1922. Photographs courtesy of BFI National Archive.

Fires of Innocence (1922)
Directed by Sidney Morgan
Cinematography by Stanley Mumford
Screenplay by Sidney Morgan
Based on the novel *A Little World Apart* by George Stevenson

Cast
Bella Blackburn – Madge Tree
Lydia Blackburn – Nell Emerald
Rev Philip Demaine – Arthur Lennard
Helen Demaine – Joan Morgan

ELECTRIC PICTURES

Arthur Demaine – Francis Innys
Mrs Ermiston – Violet Graham
Lady Crane – Marie Illington
Pen Arkwright– Bobbie Andrews
Bishop – Charles Levey

'A vivid picture of life in a rural parish ... the acting, in a story of this description, is everything and it is admirably fulfilled by Miss Joan Morgan as the daughter; particularly fine studies of the squire by Miss Marie Illington, and Mr Arthur Leonard as the kindly old clergyman, being supplied. Photography pretty, and beautifully clear. Marks 9 ½.' *The Era*, 13 September 1922.

George Stevenson, born in 1875, was a female novelist whose novels included *Topham's Folly* (1913), *Jenny Cartwright* (1914), *A Little World Apart* (1916) and *Benjy* (1919).

A Little World Apart was featured in *The New York Review of Books* (11 March 1917) where the plot is described as, 'The coming of a mysterious lady in black to the sleepy town of Applethwaite, the strange doings while she is there, the social coterie of which is for a time the centre, and her mysterious disappearance, make up the staple of this clever plot.'

In adapting Stevenson's novel for film it seems that Morgan made significant changes. A mysterious lady in black (Mrs Ermiston) does indeed appear in the sleepy village of Applethwaite. Her arrival is witnessed by two busybody sisters, Bella and Lydia Blackburn, who disapprove of this attractive widow spending time with the reverend, Philip Demaine, and report his seemingly undignified behaviour to the bishop.

But the film's star is not Violet Graham, who plays the mysterious widow, but Joan Morgan, who plays Helen Demaine, the reverend's daughter. The Demaines are an impoverished family who rely on the generous support of the squire, the 'blunt but kindly' Lady Crane. Helen is kind and supportive of her father's parish work, whereas her brother Arthur is a wastrel who repays Lady Crane's generosity by stealing one of her brooches. Helen is being wooed by Lady Crane's nephew, the dashing naval officer Pen Arkwright – which also rattles the two scandal-mongering sisters. However, when Helen spots that her father's eyesight is deteriorating she puts all thoughts of romance aside. But Lady Crane won't let her throw her life away, and is delighted when Helen and Pen become engaged. The brooch is mysteriously returned, so Arthur is safe (for now!). The bishop is persuaded that the reverend and the widow aren't an item. In fact, it transpires that the widow isn't even a widow as her husband is still alive, but suffering from shellshock. And what of the two busybody sisters? Well, despite stirring up a whole heap of trouble they are dedicated members of the Dorcas Society and have been busy hosting sewing parties, and along with Helen were instrumental in organising the Dorcas Society Bazaar, 'the event of Applethwaite's year'.

When interviewed in 1976 by historian John Montgomery, Joan Morgan reported that this was shot in September 1921. Beyond that she said, 'Oddly enough, it's the one film of which I recall *nothing* about, except Bobby [sic] Andrews!'

Twenty years later, when Joan was being interviewed by film historians Tony Fletcher and Ronald Grant, her comment on this film was, 'I remember Bobbie quite well' (clearly he made an impact!) and she added, 'we went down to Torquay to film, or Poole. I'm not quite sure'. There are some recognisable Sussex landmarks featured, including Bramber High Street doubling for Applethwaite and the Church of the Good Shepherd adjacent to the Shoreham Studios. The location of the attractive rose-garden and the arched gateway have Shoreham local history buffs stumped, so perhaps they are from the scenes shot in Devon or Dorset. Any suggestions welcomed.

Fires of Innocence reel 'found' in the BFI National Archive. (Courtesy of BFI National Archive)

Above (l-r): *Fires of Innocence* viewed on a Steenbeck; *Fires of Innocence* title credit; Nell Emerald as Lydia Blackburn in *Fires of Innocence*; Joan Morgan as Helen Demaine in *Fires of Innocence*; Marie Illington as Lady Crane in *Fires of Innocence*. (Courtesy of BFI National Archive)

Above (l-r): *Fires of Innocence*: Bobbie Andrews as Pen Arkwright looking through the windows of the Church of the Good Shepherd, Shoreham; Helen and Pen at The Dorcas Society Bazaar in *Fires of Innocence*; *Fires of Innocence*: Helen with her father, the Reverend Philip Demaine, played by Arthur Lennard; *Fires of Innocence*: Violet Graham as Mrs Ermiston and Charles Levey as the Bishop; *Fires of Innocence*: the end credit. (Courtesy of BFI National Archive)

THE DORCAS SOCIETY

The Dorcas Society is a key feature of both the novel *A Little World Apart* and the film *Fires of Innocence*. One of the earliest societies was founded in Douglas, Isle of Man, in 1834. The Dorcas Society is named after a Biblical character from the New Testament, and is seen as the 'patron of sewers'. As an organisation, they operated at both local and national levels; Dorcas Societies also focused on their role as a community group, usually linked to a church, school or mothers' group, whose main focus was to provide 'Plain and Necessary Articles of Clothing' to the poor. Although sewing machines had been in use in the domestic sphere since the 1850s, many societies continued sewing by hand, as can be seen in *Fires of Innocence* – only purchasing sewing machines once funds could be raised or were offered from donations.

Rose Sinclair, lecturer in Design (Textiles) at Goldsmiths, University of London, has written extensively on the Dorcas Society: 'Membership for even early 20th century females was still seen as a social duty to help those less fortunate whether home or abroad, particularly during times of duress or change such as war or illness. It would have probably featured in the novel and movie as a way of galvanising networks of women to create or make products for men at the front, or to help those suffering on the home front who may have suffered the loss of a husband or main earner of the family.'

8

NELL EMERALD: JEWEL OF THE SOUTH COAST MOVIELAND

BY JAMES CLARKE

When we think of silent cinema, we most readily think of the Hollywood silent film tradition that produced so many short and feature length films during the first twenty-five years of the twentieth century.

But what of British silent film stars? Well, British silent cinema had its own galaxy of stars, too. One of those stars that shone particularly brightly on the south coast was an actress whose name could not have been more fitting for stardom: Nell Emerald and her journey through both theatre and then on into the movies is a vivid reminder, and emblem, of the deep connection between the traditions of the stage and what was once upon a time the creative new world of the cinema.

The undeniable sparkle of Nell's stage name was a long way from the more modest character of her birth name: Ellen Maud O'Shea. She was born on 29 October 1882 and she would go on to lead a long and full life. Born into a theatre-world family, Nell and her four sisters were destined for the stage and sure enough they were duly billed as the 'Sisters O'Shea: Irish Duettists and Comedy Dancers'. This collective stage name was subsequently adjusted, however, courtesy of Ernest DeVere; he was the manager of Cambridge Music Hall and was keen to advertise the act with a catchier moniker. Hence, the act was rebooted as The Emerald Sisters.

Aged 28, Nell Emerald married David George Beattie (also known as Charlie), who requested that she stop her theatre work. She did so. However, her professional life took a fascinating turn as she focused on the emerging wonders and career opportunities of the film industry. Sure enough, Nell became a notable, and pioneering, film star as well as producer based on the south coast.

Nell's fellow Shoreham film star Joan Morgan recalled in later years that Nell was 'married to a very attractive and very rich bookmaker in Brighton'. (*Griffithiana*, No. 65, Oct 1999)

In her shift into the movies, Nell initially worked as one of two company directors at Brightonia Film Company, based at Hampton Street in Brighton. The operation had been established in 1913 and whilst there Nell employed two of her sisters: Monie and Eily. Nell's earliest film appearances were in *The Grip of Iron* (1914) and *A Bold Adventuress* (1915). Nell then moved to work at the Progress Film Company in Shoreham where she starred in a number of feature films produced in the early 1920s. Two of these films were amongst the most highly regarded of Progress's output: *A Lowland Cinderella* (1921), which reworked the Cinderella fairy tale, and an adaptation of the Thomas Hardy novel *The Mayor of Casterbridge* (1921), in which Nell portrayed Furmity Woman. Thomas Hardy, author of *The Mayor of Casterbridge*, even visited the Progress film studio in Shoreham during the film's production.

Recognising how fickle the entertainment industry can be when it comes to its star system, as the 1920s moved on, Nell began to focus on producing and writing. In 1933 she wrote the scenario for the Gracie Fields film, *This Week of Grace*, and, by the late 1930s, Nell had shifted out of acting and into producing.

In the 1930s, women in the British film industry typically did not have the chance to take on executive or producer roles. However, a number of women did work in a role that we might now refer to as line producer, overseeing the day-to-day production of a film. In this producer role, Nell produced a number of low-budget movies, often called 'quota quickies' with sure-to-grab-the-attention titles like *Murder at the Cabaret* (1936), *Terror on Tiptoe* (1936) and *Dr Sin Fang* (1937).

Nell's sister, Connie, would marry performer, writer and director Stanley Lupino. Their daughter, Nell's niece, was named Ida and she went on to have a fairly stunning and significant Hollywood film directing career, establishing herself as the only female director and producer working in the 1950s Hollywood studio system.

Nell died on 21 June 1969. No longer a recognised star of stage and screen, Nell was undoubtedly one of many women who blazed trails in the early years of the British film industry.

A Coda

In working on this book project, a slightly unreal-seeming, but all too true, personal connection to the film-making history of Shoreham came into focus for me. I can recall, from many years before this book project came into being, my grandma sitting in her chair and smiling as she recounted the connection between me and

52 King's Road,
Brighton.

Dear Rowland.

I thank you most sincerely for your kind words of sympathy in my recent loss.

The kindness of so many friends has done much to help me through this time of great sorrow.

Yours sincerely,

Ellen Maud Beattie.

January 1932.

P.T.O.

Nell Emerald and her sister Eily with their mother. (Courtesy of James Clarke)

Thank-you note from Nell Emerald. (Courtesy of James Clarke)

someone else on the family tree. My grandma knew all too well how much cinema meant to me.

Here's the twist of fate, then: on my mother's side of the family, the actress Nell Emerald found a place on the family tree, having married into the family which, at the time, was based in Birmingham. Here's how it threads together: Nell married Charlie Beattie and Charlie (also known as David) was my granddad's uncle. Charlie's sister was Bertha, mother to my granddad, whose name was Arthur Bowden and who was born in 1918. With this connection in mind, it's been quite moving to bring a story that's so close to home full circle. To be able to write about Nell Emerald, my great-great aunt is a special thing.

Indeed, at some time in the 1950s, Nell was in a pantomime at The Kemble Theatre on Broad Street in Hereford. My mum, to this day, clearly remembers having travelled into Hereford, with my grandad and grandma, from the outlying village where they lived, to see her great aunt performing and then also to meet her.

Not so long ago, a small collection of photographs of Nell Emerald that had been in my late grandparents' care came to light and I had the chance to look through them. In the collection is a photograph that shows Nell walking along what looks

Handwritten letter (in pencil) from Nell Emerald. (Courtesy of James Clarke)

like a pier. She is smiling and walking with her is her sister, Eily, and their mother. Bill, their mother's dog is being pushed along in what looks like a pram.

One of the other items that my mum now has to hand is a handwritten letter, put down in pencil, from Nell to her niece Daisy – my granddad Arthur's sister. Daisy was living in Birmingham. Whilst the letter is undated it does include Nell's address in Brighton: Flat 1, 54 King's Road, Brighton. Because the letter refers to a time not so long after my granddad's mother Bertha died (of a heart condition, in 1919, aged just 36) we can assume that it was written not so long thereafter. In turn, this ties in with the timeframe in which Nell worked in Brighton and Shoreham. In the letter, Nell explains that she has bought a piano for Daisy and that it would be delivered to the family home at Morley Road in Birmingham. Nell explains, too, that the piano has been mistakenly addressed to Daisy Beattie when it should have been to Daisy Bowden. In the letter, Nell also sends her best wishes to the family and makes a particular point of asking about 'little Arthur'. She signs off with 'Your ever-loving Aunty Nell. xxxx.'

It's heartening to know that Nell stayed so in touch with the family that she married into and that my mum has the happy memory of Christmas cards from Aunty Nell arriving at the house, which she grew up in near the Welsh border. Believe me when I say that a remote corner of north-west Herefordshire was such a very long way from where Aunty Nell's movie-making adventure had once upon a time sparkled and shone.

9

SHOREHAM'S LEADING LADY: JOAN MORGAN

BY ELLEN CHESHIRE

Of her father's work before becoming involved with the British film industry, Joan wrote:

> My father had a gift for writing lyrics – very good ones – and formed his own concert party. Out of these amateur beginnings he evolved as a writer and had one or two short musicals done at, I think, the London Pavilion. Once launched into this world, films, then in their exciting youth, were the next step. (*The Silent Picture*, No. 11/12, Summer/Autumn 1971)

The daughter of an actress mother, Evelyn Wood and a writer-director father, Sidney Morgan, it seemed inevitable that Joan Morgan (1905–2004) would pursue a theatrical career. Indeed, aged 5, she began going to dancing school, and made her debut at a charity show as a little Geisha. Her rise to stardom started at an early age when, aged 8, she went to New York where she was spotted by Charles Urban who cast her in the lead of *Little Lord Fauntleroy* (1913). Sadly, the film faltered when they ran foul of copyright laws, but this led to other early film roles in *The Cup Final Mystery* (1913) directed by Maurice Elvey.

At the outbreak of the First World War, Sidney sent his wife and daughter to New York, where she featured in a number of films for Fort Lee. Returning to England she appeared in her first film directed by her father, *The World's Desire* (1915), as Ellen Terry's granddaughter in *Her Greatest Performance* (1916) and in her father's film version of Emile Zola's novel *L'Assommoir* (1877), renamed *Drink* (1916), she played Gervaise as a child.

Joan Morgan. (Courtesy of John Payne)

The cast of *Little Dorrit*; Joan Morgan is in the centre. (Courtesy of the Mavis Clare/ Gillian Gregg Archive)

She recalls attending a variety of theatre schools: the Italia Conti stage school, the Tiller School of Dancing and The Vernon Castle School of Dance. She certainly made an impact on French impresario Andre Charlot who cast her in *A Pierrots' Christmas* at the Apollo Theatre on Shaftesbury Avenue and in two musical revues, *See-Saw* and *Bubbly*, the following year.

When the war ended her father began working for Progress Film Company – initially filming in Manchester and London. In summer 1919 the family took up residency at Shoreham.

She starred in eight of her father's films for Progress and other distinguished film producers of the late teens early '20s; Joan Morgan was England's film star. Whilst at Shoreham she was earning £30 a week at a time when the average salary was £400 a year. Her first film was *Lady Noggs* (1920), but it was as Amy Dorrit, in the first adaptation of Dickens's *Little Dorrit* (1920), that she was most proud. It was this film that caught the attention of Hollywood leading man, Bryant Washburn, who came to England with the intention of making Joan his leading lady. A tad surprised to find she was only 15, he still cast her in *The Road to London* (1921), in which he plays a visiting American who elopes with an heiress. This resulted in the offer of a five-year contract with Famous Players-Lasky. As she wasn't of age, her father took the meeting and turned the offer down. Seventy-five years later, when recalling her early career, Joan clearly still had regrets about this fateful decision:

> Famous Players offered me a five-year contract at $100 a week to start with. My father went up to meet them and they said 'What do you think of this offer we've made your daughter?'
>
> And he said, 'Not much.'
>
> And that was the end. You could see a complex motivation: the break-up of the family, the loss of his star and a certain amount of jealousy. And I was absolutely the type – the little soft blonde of those days – but I was only 15 – and not a pushy 15. Some girls of that age today would jump in a taxi and go. I didn't. I just died inside. (Joan Morgan in *The Independent*, 24 July 2004)

After the 1921 season Joan was offered the lead in *Swallow* (1922), Leander de Cordova's prestigous adaptation of the Rider Haggard novel, which was being shot in South Africa. 'At age 16 in Johannesburg in 1921 life was superb ... It became the most marvellous time in my life, for I still had all this wonderful career, all this money and sunlight! That was definitely the film I enjoyed making the most!' (Joan Morgan in *Classic Images* No. 178, April 1990)

Joan returned to Shoreham after the 'best five months of her life' and went straight into production of *A Lowland Cinderella* (1921), until recently thought to be the only completed Progress film. She made two more films at Progress (*The*

Lilac Sunbonnet and *Fires of Innocence*) and midway through the fourth season both she and her father left Shoreham.

The success of recent film releases including the US release of *A Lowland Cinderella* as *A Highland Maid* spurred Joan and her mother to try America again. Those few years away had clearly made a difference and she returned and took the lead in her father's production of *Shadow of Egypt (1924)* for Astra-National Productions. But when the company went to Luxor, Joan was left behind and had to recreate the desert scenes in the studio.

In 1926 her parents split up and she lived with her mother in Chelsea. Her last silent film was under the direction of her father, *A Window in Piccadilly* (1928), in which she played the daughter of a famous violinist who was played by the famous violinist Daivd DeGroot.

With the arrival of talkies her film work dried up and her last film was *Her Reputation* (1932), also directed by her father. Joan returned to the stage but was disappointed by the roles that she was being offered, as she recalled in 1995 (in an interview with Simon Fanshawe in *The Culture Magazine*, 11 June 1995): '... but there I was a rather boring type. Blondes in the theatre were "Who's for tennis?" types. The only time I got an interesting part was a cockney thief and I was terribly good!'

Like her father, Joan was a voracious reader, and had entered essay-writing competitions as a child. Therefore, a sideways move into writing seemed a natural fit. Whilst at Shoreham, Joan had gained a wider understanding of the creative side of film-making:

> I always loved the technical aspect and apart from acting and writing have been assistant director (even director for three days' shooting when my father was taken ill) and on one occasion my father left me in the cutting room with a technician and I edited an entire film, including a montage sequence of the derby. (*The Silent Picture*, No. 11/12, Summer/Autumn 1971)

Whilst acting she continued to work with her father first as a scenario writer for the silent movies, and then as a scriptwriter for early British talkies using the pseudonyms Iris North and Joan Wentworth Wood (Wood was her mother's maiden name). Most of these were for the quota quickies that had come into force in 1927, following a ten-year campaign spearheaded by her father.

Joan's most high-profile screenwriting success was *The Flag Lieutenant* (1932), directed by Herbert Wilcox, starring Anna Neagle and Henry Edwards. In the 1940s she turned to writing novels, alongside her plays, writing a total of thirteen, including *Camera!* (1940), which is set in the early days of film-making in Britain and Germany. Her last play *The Hours of Darkness* (1960), which was adapted from her novel *The Sensitive Plants* (1955), was put on in Worthing in 1960. In the 1960s she began a new career as a renovator of country houses for which she wrote the part how-to guide/part history of country houses *The Casebook of Capability Morgan* (1965). She continued to renovate properties until 1997, when aged 72 she took on her final project, a Palladian tollhouse in Henley-on-Thames, from which she enjoyed her retirement.

Little did she imagine that twenty-five years later she would be making headlines when a complete Progress film was found in America. Lost under its American release title of *A Highland Maid*, *A Lowland Cinderella* was once again back in the UK and being screened for a new generation of silent film buffs. Joan attended a special screening at Lancing College in 1996 and thought it a '… quiet sort of film. It wasn't very exciting, there wasn't a lot for me to do really. It wasn't the best.' (*Griffithiana*, October 1999)

This screening was part of the national celebrations of the Century of Cinema, for which she gave a number of press interviews and made guest appearances at events in Shoreham, including a plaque unveiling at Shoreham's Church of the Good Shepherd and an exhibition at Marlipins Museum. In 1999, aged 94, she made the journey to Northern Italy to receive a Lifetime Achievement Award at the Pordenone Silent Film Festival. In an interview with Glenda Cooper (*Mail Weekend Magazine*, 5 June 1999) Joan concluded:

> I loved *Titanic*, but the ship was the star of that. But I wouldn't have wanted Gloria Stuart's role in that film – she played Kate Winslet's character, Rose, as an older woman. You never recover as a film star, you know. Once you've finished, you're finished – the game's up and it's time to move on.

For Joan this poignant comment about a near contemporary silent film star, who like Joan had a late-in-life moment in the spotlight, is shrouded in sadness. In the same interview she once again thought about the Hollywood career that never was: 'I was terribly upset; it could have made me a Hollywood star.'

For decades, silent films were largely forgotten, ignored by audiences, film-makers, archivists and historians alike. In the 1960s this trend began to be reversed and film historians such as Rachael Low, Kevin Brownlow and Dennis Gifford began cataloguing and championing these early films. By then, however, it was estimated that 75 per cent of all silent films were lost, with figures of up to 80 per cent of British silent films being missing.

In 1914 when Joan Morgan was just beginning her foray into films, 25 per cent of films showing in the UK were thought to be British. The First World War had a crushing impact on film-making across Europe, and at the end of the war Hollywood's domination had increased to around 80 per cent of the market, leaving European countries supplying the remaining 20 per cent. In 1917 Sidney Morgan lobbied for a quota system, and in 1927 the British Government finally relinquished and established The Cinematograph Films Act of 1927, which aimed to protect the

UK industry with a quota system demanding that exhibitors show at least 5 per cent home-grown production.

Joan Morgan gave her first significant interview with Garth Peddler for *Classic Images* in 1990 when she was already 85, and her recollections don't always tally with original source material and/or one another.

One aspect of Joan Morgan's writing career was not raised in the numerous obituaries, interviews and features. I add it here as an example of Oscar Wilde's truism, in *The Critic as Artist* (1891), that 'The one duty we owe history is to re-write it'.

Whilst researching Joan Morgan in an online academic ebook repository I found her name highlighted in the sentence, 'Other contributors to the journal included A.K. Chesterton, J.F.C. Fuller, Henry Gibbs, Joan Morgan, all ex-BUF, and Rolf Gardiner.' Intrigued, I clicked on and a second quote was revealed: 'British fascists such as Joan Morgan, another BUF dissident who became involved in the New Pioneer'. Looking to the left it showed that the book these lines were from was *British Fascism, 1918–1939: Parties, Ideology and Culture* by Thomas Linehan. Could this be the same Joan Morgan? Further research proved that it was indeed the same Joan Morgan.

The British Union of Fascists (BUF) was a far-right party formed in 1932 by Oswald Mosley, which initially met with popular support and swiftly achieved a sizeable following. As the party became more radical its support declined. Its embrace of Nazi-style anti-Semitic rhetoric in 1936 led to violent confrontations, most notably in the Battle of Cable Street. The BUF subsequently changed its name in 1936 to the British Union of Fascists and National Socialists. In 1937 its name changed again to British Union. In 1940, the organisation was finally banned.

It is not clear when Joan Morgan joined the BUF, but she was publicly associated with the party once they had become more radical as she was writing for a number of their publications in 1936/7. In *The British Union Quarterly* (July–Sept 1937) she wrote an article entitled 'Can Genius Survive National Socialism?' – to which she answers in the affirmative. In 'Whither England?' (*Action,* 26 December 1936) she argues that the distress the British were currently facing was due to the effects of centuries of being the victor: 'We've been successful for so long that we still blindly believe in our ability to muddle through.'

But it is her article 'Who has Ruined British Films?' (*Action*, 23 January 1937) that is most damning. Here she credits the industrial British technicians, writers, actors, but questions why they are often overlooked in favour of 'second-rate American stars' being paid such vast salaries as £1,000 a week, and asks 'where – and I ask it in all sincerity – is the honest cleverness of these Jews?' She returns to this theme later when querying the high salaries of the 'second-rate American stars' and the 'profit of the Hollywood Jew agents'.

She also berates the influx of actors fleeing Germany and their high salaries, who have:

no better artistic record in Berlin than a host of our own directors and artists who know nothing of our customs and conditions ... Meanwhile our own men and women, who have devoted their lives to the development of a new industry in Britain, are condemned to the Quota slough and begging favours of men who were their employees ten years ago, or in extreme cases, poverty, suicide and death from broken hearts.

She ends the piece by saying: 'It has been stated that most film magnates graduated from the fur trade. Any trade with money in it is equally good for the Jews. Let them leave the Film Industry to the men and women whose life-blood it is, that splendid legion of British workers whose love for it is so deep that they never complain at 24-hour days.'

This revelation certainly offers an alternate reading and a more complex understanding of the end of her film-acting career in 1932.

CAMERA! (1940)

'*Camera!* is my history of the British film industry as I knew it. It takes us right back to the very early days of a child actress, and there is quite a bit in it about Berlin. It isn't really an autobiography. It is entirely a fictitious story as regards backgrounds and so on, going right up to the end of the silent era with a wonderful film into which they had been putting all their hearts and souls called *Faust*. This, I might as well now reveal, wasn't meant to be Murnau's *Faust*, not a compatible film like Galeen's *The Student of Prague* (which were both 1926 films), but really Viatcheslav Tourjansky's *Volga! Volga!* of 1928.' (Joan Morgan, *Classic Images*, no. 180, June 1990)

Camera! (Courtesy of the Ronald Grant Archives)

10

THE STAR OF CASTERBRIDGE: MAVIS CLARE AND HER PROGRESSION WITH PROGRESS

BY JAMES CLARKE

Shoreham's film studio scene was home to not only female film stars Joan Morgan and Nell Emerald but also to Mavis Clare.

Just as Joan Morgan, who took the lead in eight Progress films, was the daughter of Sidney Morgan, so too was Mavis Clare the beneficiary of the family business when her father Frank Spring cast her in several films, starting with smaller roles before graduating to star parts when Joan left Progress to work for other film producers.

Born on 9 April 1905, Mavis Clare (her actual name was Kathleen Spring) had a small role in *Little Dorrit* and appears in *A Lowland Cinderella* as Ethel Torpichan, one of bad Dr Torpichan's daughters

It's Clare's role as Elizabeth in the Progress adaptation of Thomas Hardy's novel *The Mayor of Casterbridge* for which she should be perhaps best known, however. The film is considered a considerable achievement and it was for this film that Kathleen Spring became Mavis Clare.

Of Mavis, Joan Morgan, writing in 1976 to film historian John Montgomery, commented that '[Mavis] was very pretty and made two or three films'.

The Mayor of Casterbridge (1922) was Sidney Morgan's last film for Progress. It was made whilst Joan was filming on location in South Africa in a film version of Rider Haggard's *Swallows*. It was filmed partly in Dorset and made with the full endorsement of Thomas Hardy who visited location filming at Dorchester. Sidney Morgan had been really keen to secure Hardy's approval before filming and sent the script to him ahead of production. Hardy said of the script that it was 'as good as is compatible with presentation by cinemas'. (*Seeing Hardy: Film and Television Adaptations of the Fiction of Thomas Hardy*, Date: 251) Author Paul J. Niemeyer, author of *Seeing Hardy*, commented: 'This adaptation concentrates on Henchard's relationship with Elizabeth Jane. Whereas the novel is set in the 1840s the film suggests a late nineteenth/early twentieth century setting.'

Gillian Gregg, daughter of Mavis Clare, donated what might best be described as a treasure trove of information and material to Screen Archive South East (SASE) where it's now registered as the Gillian Gregg Archive. *Little Dorrit* and *The Mayor of Casterbridge* are each archived, albeit as partial films only, at Screen Archive South East.

Mavis Clare. (Courtesy of the Mavis Clare/ Gillian Gregg Archive)

MY MUM, THE FILM STAR
BY GILLIAN GREGG

Firstly let me say that I adored my mum. This photo was taken of us in August 1936, twelve years after her filming days came to an end. She married my dad in 1933 at the age of 28.

I did not find out about 'The Progress Film Co.' started by my grandfather, and all the films that were made in Shoreham-by-Sea, until I was well in my teens. Sadly she never talked much about those years and I so regret not asking and finding out more whilst my grandparents and mum were still alive. When I said I would love to see the films, I was told they had all been burnt in a fire.

It was only after she died that I discovered my mum had kept a wonderful collection of memorabilia with albums of photographs and newspaper cuttings. I learnt so much more about their time in Bungalow Town, and realised it had obviously been a special time in her life and meant a lot to her.

However, all her life she had a problem about anyone knowing her age! I believe this was because she was five years older than my dad. When looking at some of the photos in the albums I noticed that the dates were all crossed out and am sure this was to conceal her age from anyone looking at them.

I do wonder what my mum and grandfather would think if they knew there was so much interest in their filming days on Shoreham beach nearly a 100 years ago! They would be astounded.

Mum was very kind and fun loving, and I have so many precious memories of her.

Mavis Clare and Gillian Gregg in 1936.
(Courtesy of Gillian Gregg family archive)

11

ON THE BORDER: WHAT A COASTAL SETTING MIGHT MEAN

BY JAMES CLARKE

Films shot in Worthing and Shoreham

There's something very particular about the English south coast: it's not only a physical edge but often, too, a place where human behaviour arrives at its limit. The coast and its seaside towns have the capacity to become something of a borderland or perhaps even a hinterland between the routine and mundane, and the novel and the unusual. The rules that typify the day-to-day roll out with the tide.

The coast is where dreams can be searched out and realised. Is it too much of an imaginative stretch, therefore, to make the comparison between the 'dreamland' of southern California and the stretch of sea, beach and blue skies that makes for the West Sussex coast?

Here, then, is a guide to films that have showcased Shoreham and Worthing over the past fifty years. The films referenced in this section put Shoreham or Worthing on screen; either for just a fleeting instance or for a more sustained moment of movie-glory. Either way, immortality is assured.

Films

The Birthday Party (1968)

Harold Pinter's 1957 stage play *The Birthday Party* tells the simmering, claustrophobic story of a man named Webster who takes lodgings in a sleepy seaside town, only to find himself intimidated by two other newly arrived boarders. It transpires that Webster has deserted from a criminal gang and the newly arrived lodgers have come to find him. In writing the play, Pinter drew on his own memories of staying in a seaside boarding house whilst working as an actor in a touring play.

One poster for the film's UK release included a block of text that reads: 'Robert Shaw in Harold Pinter's gripping horror comedy.' William Friedkin, who directed the film adaptation, said in an interview with *Venice Magazine* in 1997: 'The Birthday Party ... was a great experience ... Pinter was on the set all the time. Very supportive.'

The film star Robert Shaw played Stanley Webster, and the two gang members, McCann and Goldberg, were played by Patrick Magee and Sydney Tafler respectively. Dandy Nichols and Moultrie Kelsall played the characters Petey and Meg, the down-at-heel owners of the boarding house in which the drama tautly unfolds.

Famously, Friedkin's film adaptation of the book ended with two scenes that were shot in Worthing. In establishing a sense of place, the scenes capture the lurking potential for something unsettling to occur. The exterior of the house was filmed on Eriswell Road, which runs north to south from Shelley Road to Rowlands Road.

The Birthday Party has become something of a minor movie classic. *The New York Times* commented on the film's opening scene (shot in Worthing): 'Friedkin captures in simple visual terms the verbalised purgatory of Pinter's play. There is both the hint of menace, never defined, and the suggestion of the dislocation of familiar things, which can be both terrifying and funny.' In a review that was written some years after the film's original release, *Time Out* magazine (date unknown) called the film a 'flashy piece of seaside gothic'. To this day, *The Birthday Party* remains a cult film.

Up the Junction (1968)

Directed by Peter Collinson and produced by Anthony Havelock-Allan and John Brabourne, this is the film adaptation, rather than the Ken Loach TV adaptation of 1965, of Nell Dunn's novel (taken from a series published in *The New Statesman* in 1963) of the same name, in which a middle-class young woman named Polly (Suzy Kendall) moves from the comfortable surrounds of her family's home in Chelsea to Battersea, on the south side of the River Thames. As the crow flies, Battersea is no great distance from Chelsea at all, and yet it's a world away in many other respects. The title of the book refers to Clapham Junction railway station in south London: a junction that brings travellers in and out of London and southwards to the south coast.

In Battersea, Polly meets Peter (Dennis Waterman), 19 years old and already tired of the south London life that Polly now finds so interesting. Sure enough, their relationship becomes more complicated and at a critical moment in the drama, Peter takes Polly away for a weekend to the south coast. By this point in the story the trip is a way of escaping the pressures of life in Battersea and, for Peter, once on the coast he is able to ask Polly a question. Whereas Waterman was a familiar face from plenty of stage and TV appearances, Suzy Kendall was a new talent to most viewers. The film's cast also included Adrienne Posta, Maureen Lipman and Liz Fraser.

By the time that *Up the Junction* was adapted, Dunn had published three novels, which were also adapted.

A subplot in the film explores the subject of abortion – Polly accompanies a newly made friend to an abortionist.

The film was shot on location on the prom at Worthing and this setting is showcased in a scene that shows Peter and Polly driving towards the pier. We see Peter looking at the hotels along the seafront as he sits at the steering wheel and we then see Peter and Polly pull up outside the hotel where they plan to enjoy their weekend away. The hotel is now the Travelodge on Marine Parade.

In one scene, Peter is shown ordering jellied eels. The fleeting moment includes a shot from inside the cabin looking out towards Worthing Pier looking resplendent in the sunshine.

It's fair to say that *Up the Junction* remains a compelling drama that is very clearly of its time. When originally released, *The New York Times* in its review of 14 March 1968 made a point of highlighting Dennis Waterman's performance: 'There is a really beautiful piece of characterisation by Dennis Waterman.' For the film's cinema release the poster campaign included the following, somewhat unsubtle, tagline: '"Don't get caught" was what she wasn't taught.'

The Rise and Rise of Michael Rimmer (1970)

Directed by Kevin Billington, produced by Tommy Thompson and executive produced by David Frost this satirical film is about a pollster and political maven who becomes prime minister. The film was the brainchild of David Frost and was joined on the project by Graham Chapman and John Cleese – whom some would know from the TV series *Monty Python's Flying Circus* and, prior to that, the satirical show *That Was The Week That Was*. We might judge the film to be all the more pertinent today when image (or the idea of being 'on message') and reality don't always line up.

The film stars Peter Cook, who, at the time of the film's production, was a major star of TV comedy and who was, and continues to be considered, one of Britain's great comedians. Cook and the film's director Kevin Billington co-wrote the screenplay with Chapman and Cleese.

It's quite telling that the film has enjoyed new interest in recent years: in 2010 it was included in the Edinburgh International Film Festival strand entitled 'After the Wave: Lost and Forgotten British Cinema, 1967–1979'. Nick Fulton, who programmed the strand, said of the film that its comedy is really about 'the idea of the British national identity being challenged by diversity'. (*Sight and Sound*, July 2010). Could such a statement be more true than today?

Filmed partly on location in Worthing, the film includes a scene in which a pollster named Crodder is seen walking down a Worthing residential street. We see a character named Pumer (John Cleese) at an unknown location along the riverside. A scene featuring Peter Cook and Denholm Elliot and Ronald Fraser was filmed on Worthing Pier, which doubles, as it has done on a number of occasions, as Brighton Pier.

The film was a disaster both commercially and critically, and Peter Cook's nascent film career never really recovered. John Cleese, who appears in the film, noted that Cook's comic skills were best suited to the sketch format rather than the long arc of a film storyline.

Dance with a Stranger (1985)
Dance with a Stranger dramatises the true story of Ruth Ellis, the last woman to be hanged in Britain. Playing the role of Ruth Ellis, Miranda Richardson is now something of a household name to audiences – this was the film that put Richardson on the movie map.

Directed by Mike Newell, *Dance with a Stranger* is a compelling slice of British movie realism that also pleasingly trades on a number of film noir conventions. The film explores Ellis's ultimately doomed relationship with racing driver David Blakely (Rupert Everett). The film also features Ian Holm as Desmond Cussen, Ruth's 'sugar daddy'.

Marine Parade in Worthing enjoys a dash of on-screen glory in a scene in which Ruth and Desmond go to the seaside for a picnic with her young son, Andy. A nicely framed mid shot in the scene shows Desmond and Ruth looking out to sea with Worthing Pier and Pavilion Theatre in the background – conjuring something of the tendency for seaside resorts to delight in architecture that's just that bit larger than life. A subsequent medium close-up shows Ruth and Desmond looking at Andy (off screen) that incorporates Worthing's Dome Cinema in the background. In this same sequence, we see Ruth posing for pictures to be taken by Desmond on the beach, his obsession with Ruth manifested in his picture taking.

An essential British movie of its era, *Dance with a Stranger* enjoyed terrific reviews. The Film4 website reviews the film: 'A powerful and evocative drama, which doesn't flinch in its depiction of a tragic, abusive affair.' *Time Out* magazine, in a review in 1985, said of the film: 'What the movie captures perfectly is the seedy mood of repression, so characteristic of austerity Britain in the '50s.'

Wish You Were Here (1987)

Like *Dance with a Stranger*, this movie is key to the British cinema of the 1980s and it's hugely important to the history of Worthing as a notable film location. The film captures that classic, even iconic, south-coast vibe that is typical of the places in and around Worthing. Worthing is to *Wish You Were Here* what New York is to the film *Breakfast at Tiffany's*.

Wish You Were Here tells the story of a young woman named Lynda who lives on the south coast of England, in the years following the Second World War. There's a striking sense of dreariness that the film conjures, into which Lynda brings some much-needed playfulness. In a conversation for this book, the film's writer-director, David Leland, recalled the process of settling on a location for the film: 'At one point, [production designer] Caroline Amies and I went to the Isle of Wight because it had a 1950s feel to it and it was only on the ferry back that I said "What if there was a ferry strike?" We decided to rule out the Isle of Wight and that was when we looked at Worthing.' (David Leland, July 2016)

Recalling his process of scouting out potential locations for the film, David Leland recalls: 'What I did initially was a recce on my own of the whole South Coast, and I just drove, looking for key places and back streets and then I did the same route again later on with (producer) Sarah Radcliffe, putting it together in our heads.'

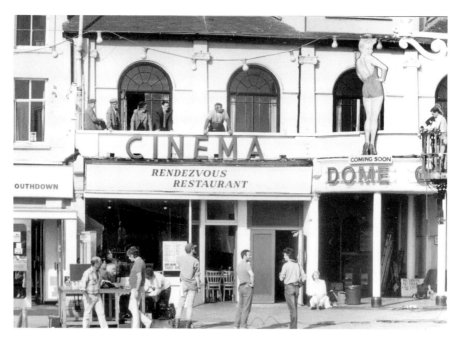

Construction work being carried out for the filming of *Wish You Were Here* outside the Dome Cinema. (West Sussex Past)

In the story, Lynda's dad, Hubert Mansell, owns a shop and for those scenes featuring the location, the production shot its material on Rowlands Road in Worthing. During a flashback scene we see Lynda and her younger sister outside their family home festooned with Union Jacks and bunting soon after the end of the Second World War. This scene was filmed on York Road in Worthing. There's then a subsequent shot in which we see Hubert returning home from war in his naval uniform and this key moment was filmed on York Road, looking towards Marine Parade. A later scene in the back garden was filmed on York Road.

In the film, Lynda starts a new job at a local bus company. This was filmed on location at Southdown Garage, Library Place in Worthing. For a scene in which Hubert watches Lynda cycle down an alleyway behind their home, the production filmed in an alleyway off Alfred Place in Worthing. As Lynda cycles along, there is a shot of her passing a character named Uncle Brian and this moment was filmed on Chesswood Road in Worthing. The house behind the gate that Lynda cycles past is no longer to be found there. Another job that Lynda takes on is serving fish and chips and there is a marvellous wide shot that showcases the stretch of the beach at Worthing at Splash Point, looking eastward late in the day. Following the moment when Lynda leaves home and goes to Eric at the Dome Cinema, there is a shot that's framed from a high vantage point that shows Lynda walking down the steps at Marine Parade with the sea and the pier behind her. We are then shown her destination and we see Lynda walking towards the doorway of the Dome Cinema on Marine Parade. The camera then tilts up to show the Dome logo in neon, and there above it a striking cut-out of Hollywood film star Betty Grable.

It's important to note here that the Dome Cinema has been restored in the decades since the film was made.

Of the presence of the Dome Cinema in the film, David Leland recalled in conversation for this book in July 2016:

> For me, the cinema is important: the Dome was a pretty important discovery because, in writing the film, I just had Tom Bell's character lodging in a room. But, the designer looked, she investigated the tower: we came up into the room inside the tower for the scene where Tom Bell rapes Lynda.

A later shot, with the camera high up above the Dome rooftop, looking down, shows Eric leaving the cinema and stepping out onto Marine Parade. Marine Parade then features in a scene in which Lynda poses for a photo with her fellow waitresses: this moment in the movie was filmed on what had originally been the entrance to Warnes Hotel, Marine Parade. Indeed, this hotel also features in *Up the Junction*. The hotel burnt down in 1987 and on its site were built luxury apartments.

The film concludes with Lynda pushing a pram as she walks back towards home, her striking yellow dress contrasting boldly with the muted surroundings of York Road and Alfred Place.

When *The Los Angeles Times* reviewed the film on 30 July 1987, it pointedly observed that, 'Leland has a reason, a purpose, a history for every character – and for every claustrophobic brick-row house or damp, echoing picture palace.' Now, in 2016, the film enjoys a new lease of life as it's one of the first titles to be made available via Film4's newly launched online film archive.

Television

It's not only feature films that have embraced the visual appeal of Worthing and Shoreham's coastal settings. Television drama and television comedy has repeatedly offered up views of the towns and sometimes to very memorable effect.

Men Behaving Badly – Series 6, episode 3 'Gary In Love' (1998)
In this episode of the very successful BBC 1990s British sitcom that embraced the idea of lad culture as a 20-something man, Gary (Martin Clunes) heads to Worthing on business. Inevitably, he is soon joined by his friends Tony (Neil Morrissey), Dorothy (Caroline Quinn) and Deborah (Leslie Ash).

The Dome features in a scene shot at nighttime as Gary and Tony drink on the crazy golf course. On the pier, Gary realises that he is in love with Dorothy.

Cor, Blimey! (2000)
The cheeky sense of humour that's traditionally been a part of the seaside holiday sensibility fits just perfectly with a particularly British film tradition: the iconic series of *Carry On* films make a perfect fit with the British seaside. *Cor, Blimey!* tells the story of the relationship between two stars of the *Carry On* films: Barbara Windsor and Sid James. Geoffrey Hutchings portrays Sid and Samantha Spiro portrays Barbara Windsor.

The TV film is an adaptation by its writer-director Terry Johnson of his own 1988 National Theatre stageplay *Cleo, Camping, Emmanuelle and Dick*. Of the film, Johnson commented at the time of its broadcast: 'One of the ironies is the abject misery most comedians seem to go through towards the end of their lives.'

In the film, Worthing features but is in fact standing in for Brighton for a sequence that recreates some of the filming that was undertaken for *Carry On Girls*. Worthing Pier also features for a scene between Barbara and Sid.

The Fear (2012) – Channel 4 drama series

There's a rich tradition of the south-coast crime story, most famously embodied just along the coast in the form of *Brighton Rock*, but also the countless British B-movies of the 1950s. *The Fear*, written by Richard Cottan, did a compelling job of mining this combustible combination. The series starred Peter Mullan as a Brighton-based crime boss named Richie Beckett who finds himself in the throes of early onset dementia.

Whilst set in Brighton, *The Fear*'s production team used Worthing Pier to stand in for Brighton Pier as they found it a more photogenic location. It's worth saying, too, that certain shots filmed in Worthing had their backgrounds replaced, using visual effects, with an image of the Brighton seafront.

Cuffs (2015)

Cuffs was a short-lived, eight-episode BBC venture that only enjoyed one series, first broadcast on BBC1 in autumn 2015 and cancelled to the annoyance of its swiftly formed fan base.

Conceived by writer Julie Gearey, *Cuffs* was a contemporary take on the well-established TV formula that combines the police procedural drama with dramas about the police officers' private and personal lives. Key to the distinction of *Cuffs* was the way that it foregrounded its specifically south-coast setting. Indeed, in preparing the series, the scripts were as much informed by the storylines of the characters as by the production team's numerous visits in autumn 2014 to Worthing and Adur in order to gauge how a particular place could shape a plot.

Filming locally in spring 2015, *Cuffs* (whilst set in Brighton) made use of a number of very recognisable locations in and around Worthing.

In an interview with the *Shoreham Herald* in April 2015, the series location manager Peter-Frank Dewulf commented that, 'Worthing is actually a lot more film friendly than Brighton. So most of the filming of the interiors is done in the Worthing and Adur area …'

Teville Gate (multi-storey car park), the Castle Tavern in Newland Road, Portland House in Richmond Road and Long Fend Foods in Southwick Square all appear in the series. Worthing Town Hall was used as a courtroom.

Shoreham Port also features as a location and Adur Civic Centre on Ham Road, Shoreham, featured in every episode as the setting for the police station. The ground floor became the cellblock and custody suite, and the first floor was used for office scenes.

The cast of *Cuffs* included Ashley Walters, Peter Sullivan, Amanda Abbington, Shaun Dooley, Paul Ready, Eleanor Matsuura and Alex Carter. *Cuffs* also introduced Jacob Ifan in his first leading television role.

In its 28 October 2015 review of *Cuffs*, *The Independent* commented that the coastal setting 'made for a fresh feeling backdrop'.

Films on Shoreham Harbour, Beach and Fort

Ghost Ship (1952)

One of the qualities that defines life on the coast, right there on the edge of everything, is that sense of being removed from the day-to-day routines of the rest of the world. Taking this to heart, some film-makers have recognised the opportunity offered by the coast's potential as a place of spooks and scares. Film director Vernon Sewell owned a yacht and made good on its potential as a film location whilst moored at Shoreham Harbour.

The poster for *Ghost Ship*, with its lurid font and visual design, includes the promise of scares with its gleefully unsubtle tagline: 'DEAD MEN SPEAK to solve the secret of this dreaded devil-yacht!' Vernon Sewell specialised in horrors, comedies, dark thrillers and B-movies (or second features as they are also called). Sewell's movies are an important contribution to the history of the often rather neglected British B-movie tradition and to the horror film cycle that British cinema made something of a mark in through the 1950s and on into the late '60s.

Partly filmed on location aboard Sewell's yacht as a means of maximising its low B-movie budget, *Ghost Ship* tells the story of a newlywed couple, Guy and Margaret Thornton (played by Dermot Walsh and Hazel Court) who, upon buying a luxury yacht, are duly warned of its questionable history. This is a simply structured ghost story that, alas, is not especially cinematic. The production's low budget really

Shoreham Harbour in *Ghost Ship* (1952).

does show in the uninteresting framing and staging of action. For trivia buffs, Ian Carmichael and Joss Ackland both appear in the film. For all of its inadequacies, *Ghost Ship* stands as a curio – a minor example of the B-movie tradition in Britain in the years after the Second World War.

The Flaw (1955)

How tightly bound the crime genre has become with the British south coast. Directed by Terrence Fisher, who would go on to be so essential to the Hammer horror movies of the late 1950s and '60s, *The Flaw* is a low-budget crime piece, and its premise turns on a racing driver named Paul Oliveri (John Bentley) who plots to kill his wife and claim the insurance money. However, the lawyer for Oliveri's wife is in love with her and he duly uncovers his plan and the drama builds towards a fight between lawyer and racing driver.

The film was one of many B-movies made for the British film industry where these 'second features' supported the A-feature so that audiences would watch a newsreel, a second feature and then the main attraction.

In the middle of the film, Oliveri arrives at a house in Southaven and surprises the housekeeper. This exterior was shot on location at Kingston Bay Road in Shoreham-by-Sea. A subsequent scene then follows in which we see Oliveri dragging a sack containing the body of Millway from the back of the house towards the beach. This, again, was shot at Shoreham-by-Sea.

Hell Drivers (1957)

Hell Drivers, what a title for a movie and what a tagline on its poster too: 'They fight to the death and the weapons are ten ton trucks!' The film was written and directed by C.Y. Endfield and was based on a short story by John Kruse. Apparently, the short story in turn was prompted by an actual event. Whilst the title might suggest the promise of some kind of grindhouse horror, *Hell Drivers* is in fact a minor classic of the British crime movie genre that tells the story of an ex-convict (Tom) who gets work with a haulage company and exposes a racket being run by the boss and his best driver (Red). The film builds towards a truck race and chase that culminates at Shoreham. The film's cast features the stars of its day and also a couple of actors who would go on to become household names: Stanley Baker portrays the film's clean cut hero Tom and Patrick McGoohan portrays his nemesis, Red.

The cast of *Hell Drivers* is rounded out by Herbert Lom, Sid James, Alfie Bass, Gordon Jackson, Peggy Cummings and Jill Ireland. The film's cast also includes a young and unknown actor named Sean Connery.

Hell Drivers is a fascinating example of how a genre film can hit all of the required storytelling buttons, in this case working as a crime drama, whilst also providing a shot of social commentary in the grand British film tradition.

BLAZING TRUCK 'PAY-OFF' ON TRULEIGH HILL

Deliberately crashed into quarry – for a film!

A scene of a lorry aflame going over a cliff was filmed at Truleigh Hill, which is just north of Shoreham. In the *Shoreham Herald*, in 1957, a local news story covered the location filming. A photo shows a lorry plummeting off the edge of the quarry featured in the article. A second photo shows the crashed lorry accompanied by the comment, 'In the foreground are the producer Mr C.Y. Endfield, and some of his assistants. It will be some time before the "meaty" film is released for general exhibition.'

THIS IS THE "PAY-OFF" in the new film "Hell's Drivers', which the Rank Organisation completed at Truleigh Hill this week Above is the "bad man's" lorry shooting over the edge of a quarry to death and destruction. Below, the end of a thrilling shot The "villain" has met his doom. In the foreground are the producer Mr Cy Endfield, and some of his assistants. It will be some time before the "meaty" film is released for general exhibition.

The film was promoted very much around the image of speeding lorries and in the promotional campaign for the film one of the advertising slogans says: 'These are the Hell Drivers. Men with shadowy pasts dicing with death on dangerous roads.' Phew! An interesting facet of the film's marketing campaign was that the film distributor commissioned the creation of a short comic strip that comprised five parts and was made available to local papers in the UK.

Rogue's Yarn (1956)

Vernon Sewell, B-movie film directing ace of Shoreham, wrote and directed this quite well-regarded crime thriller, in which a man named John Marsden (played by Derek Bond) murders his wife Hester (played by Nicole Manvey) and then tries to put together an alibi that he hopes will dupe the authorities. However, Marsden finds himself being relentlessly pursued by a detective (played by Elwyn Brook-Jones) as the action moves back and forth between Shoreham and Le Havre.

Certainly, the film offers a number of shots in which the comings and goings of activity in Shoreham Harbour add a welcome hint of local colour.

The Battle of the V1 (1958)

The director of *The Battle of the V1* was Vernon Sewell, the 'movie auteur' of Shoreham. This movie was an adaptation of the book *They Saved London* written by Bernard Newman.

Described in its advertising campaign as 'An Epic Film Tribute to the RAF and the Polish Resistance', the film is set during the Second World War in which two Polish resistance fighters are on a mission to smuggle plans of a secret Nazi flying missile.

A low-budget film, Sewell incorporates into his footage elements from existing documentary footage in newsreels. The low budget for the film is also belied in some of the costume choices that result in various inaccuracies in terms of the rank of given soldiers and the uniforms that they wear. Perhaps the most interesting piece of trivia about this film is that the late, great Christopher Lee appears as an SS officer.

The film was shot on location at Shoreham Beach and at Shoreham Harbour for scenes that were set in a concentration camp. Scenes of armoured trucks in action were also filmed near Shoreham Harbour.

Shadow of Fear (1963)

Directed by Ernest Morris for the Butcher's Film Service, the film is a take on the enduring crime genre: it's a lovers-on-the-run movie about a couple who hide out in Seaford. Seaford is east of Shoreham and Worthing, en route to Eastbourne, but some of the film was shot at Shoreham Harbour.

Southwick (Brighton B power station) was a building that was duly demolished in two phases: in 1988 and 1998 and at the end of this film we can see Albion Street in Southwick.

Smokescreen (1964)

A standard issue British B-movie that was filmed largely in Brighton (including at a very small film studio facility there) but which also headed west to Shoreham for a few brief moments of location filming.

The film is about a very conscientious insurance assessor named Roper who travels to Brighton to investigate a potential fraud case. In doing so, a murder is uncovered.

The film, shot on location on Gardner Road in Shoreham, shows Roper and his colleague, Bayliss, driving to a factory as part of their investigations. The tell-tale sign that it's Southwick is the chimney stack of Shoreham power station seen poking out over the rooftops of the houses on Gardner Road.

This is a rather warmly regarded B-film and of its appeal, the BFI have commented that, 'What really elevates *Smokescreen* above the morass of British B-films is Peter

Vaughan's lead performance (demonstrating the way second features could offer middle-aged character actors opportunities that were denied elsewhere).'

Resort to Murder (1995)

Directed by Bruce MacDonald and written by Tony McHale, this five-part series with the excellent title had something of a tangled and tortured route to the screen. Considered as a major BBC crime drama, when the filming had been completed and the series edited, commissioning editors at the BBC thought that they had a series on their hands that was too complex in plotting and with too many dips into less popular ways of shooting a scene. Indeed, the difficulties of the production were charted by *The Independent* in an article published in July 1995.

Black Sea (2014)

A major movie shot for just two days on location at Shoreham Harbour in autumn 2013 for scenes towards the end of the film when the submarine is found by divers. Starring Jude Law, the film is about a treasure hunt by a submarine crew for gold in the Black Sea.

A *Shoreham Herald* news story describes the filming and the report includes the following detail: 'Philip Ayton, treasurer of Shoreham Sailing Club, said: "The film crew needed a safe and relatively private launching ramp for their RIBs, and our club facilities just near the harbour entrance were the obvious location."'

Filming at Shoreham Airport

Shoreham Airport is a highlight of British aviation art-deco era architectural history. It's the oldest airport in the UK and is now a Grade II Listed building. It was opened in 1910 and is a testament to the romance of aviation that characterised its earliest years. In 1934–35, the airport added a terminal building, designed by Stavers Hessel Tiltman and constructed by James Bodel Ltd, that was opened in 1936 and that was notable for its appropriately exotic sounding 'fly-in bar and restaurant'.

Its well-maintained buildings and grounds and relatively close proximity to London make it an ideal location for period dramas.

The Battle of the V1 (1958) shot some of its material here.

The Body Stealers (1969) was a science fiction detective movie in which two investigators try to uncover why paratroopers are vanishing mid air. Their sleuthing eventually reveals an alien is plotting to steal earthlings.

Shoreham Airport features for the film's closing scene in which, with the mystery solved, the character of Megan flies off.

Climping Beach also features in the film for a scene in which Megan meets Lorna.

Poirot
The hugely successful British series showcased Shoreham Airport in three episodes ('The Adventure of the Western Star' (1990), 'Death in the Clouds' (1992) and 'Lord Edgware Dies' (2000)), in which it doubled for Croydon Airport in Surrey. Shoreham Airport's appeal is easily recognised: the terminal building is a Grade II art-deco building that was listed in 1984. As such, for many people Shoreham Airport still retains that magical quality associated with the romance of early civil aviation when suddenly the world was only a plane ride away.

Richard III (1995)
This is a highly regarded adaptation of William Shakespeare's play, directed by Richard Loncraine with Ian McKellen as Richard. It updates the story to an unsettling version of England in the 1930s, and Shoreham Airport features for those scenes that are set at an aerodrome.

The Da Vinci Code (2006)
In this hugely successful film based on the bestselling novel of the same name by Dan Brown, Shoreham Airport features fleetingly as our heroes Langdon, Sophie and Teabing outwit the bad guys who are trying to find the Holy Grail before they do. Shoreham Airport is named as Le Bourget Airport in France and it's from here that the Grail seekers head for London.

Shoreham Airport dressed for the Second World War scenes from *Woman in Gold* (2015).

Woman in Gold (2015) stars Helen Mirren and Ryan Reynolds in a story based on a real incident in which Maria Altmann, a Holocaust survivor, went to court in the 1980s to reclaim five stolen Gustav Klimt paintings. The film includes scenes set during the Second World War and it's for this part of the film that Shoreham Airport is showcased. The location doubles as Nazi-era Vienna, swastika flags, German planes and period cars helping set the timeframe. The production shot for just one day at Shoreham Airport in summer 2014. Of the location, the film's director, Simon Curtis, said in an interview dated 10 April 2015 with the *Bognor Regis Observer* that, 'It is a very beautiful period airport.'

There was even a dose of controversy during filming when people arrived at Shoreham for D-Day celebrations only to find the airport festooned in Nazi-themed set decoration. In somewhat melodramatic fashion, the *Daily Mail* reported: 'Pictures from the scene also showed two swastika flags erected just metres from a war memorial' (5 June 2014). A local resident was quoted in the article saying that, 'Clearly no consideration was made to the sensitivity of locals and residents around here. Lots of people just couldn't believe it.'

The Crown filmed at the airport on 23 November 2015. This news series for Netflix is about Queen Elizabeth II's connections with the political establishment. The series was written by Peter Morgan who is notable as the screenwriter of *The Queen*, *Frost/Nixon* and *The Damned United*. The scene shot at the airport featured John Lithgow as Winston Churchill.

Vernon Sewell: Auteur of Shoreham

By James Clarke

Vernon Sewell might be described as a British B-movie maven. It might be fair to say that to even the more well-informed film enthusiasts his name is not easily recognised or referenced.

Most of the feature films that he directed were never major film releases. That said, Sewell did make a handful of contributions to the British horror and crime genres and his career spanned a significant period of mid-twentieth-century British film and TV production.

Sewell began his long-running British film and TV career as an assistant camera-man at Walton Studios and through the 1930s worked as an art director and film editor. Sewell's debut feature as director was written by none other than Michael Powell and was called *The Medium* (1934).

Sewell then continued his association with Powell, working as a production assistant on Powell's film *The Edge of the World* (1937). Sewell's film *The Silver Fleet* (1943), a production for Powell's company The Archers, really put Sewell on the film industry map as a director. Sewell co-directed the film with Gordon Wellesley and it told the true story of a Dutch shipbuilder who pretended to be loyal to Germany in order to disguise his involvement with the British.

Sewell then segued from war movie to horror movie when he directed *Latin Quarter* (aka *Frenzy*, 1947) in which a sculptor with a killer instinct hides his victims in his sculptures. This film was a solid hit and Sewell then directed the comedy *The Ghosts of Berkeley Square* (1947), starring Robert Morley and Felix Aylmer. However, when this movie didn't prove so popular Sewell's foray into A-movies came to an end and he shifted into, and remained working in, the British B-movie world that would thrive during the 1950s.

Sewell directed three thrillers in the early 1960s that have garnered what we might call a cult following: crime piece *The Man in the Back Seat* (1960), horror piece *House of Mystery* (1961) and another crime piece entitled *Strongroom* (1962). Sewell would go on to direct the horror films *Curse of the Crimson Altar* (1968) that starred Boris Karloff, Christopher Lee and Barbara Steele and *The Blood Beast Terror* (1968). Sewell would also work on one episode of *The Avengers* as an assistant director.

There's a welcome tradition in film history of film-makers becoming synonymous with specific locations. In terms of British cinema we readily might think of the connection between Michael Powell and the Kent landscape and of David Lean with the northern landscape of *Brief Encounter*. More modestly than those very high-profile examples, for Vernon Sewell his creative muse was somewhat sparked by Shoreham Harbour and the yacht that he kept moored there. In thriftily inventive fashion, which suited the B-movie scale that he typically worked on, Sewell found ways to incorporate his yacht into the scenarios of several films that he directed. In his own low-budget way, Vernon Sewell rendered Shoreham Harbour a twilight zone of sorts for the movie screen.

Sewell's yacht features as a notable location in *Ghost Ship* (1952), *The Floating Dutchman* (1953) and *Dangerous Voyage* (1954). Whilst these films may never be considered major accomplishments they are important in terms of the role played by Shoreham and Worthing in British film history.

Ghost Ship tells the tale of a newly married couple who discover that the yacht they have bought isn't quite the dreamboat they were expecting. This unadorned ghost story isn't the most dynamic movie but its lo-fi charm offers some interest and it features screen appearances by Joss Ackland and Ian Carmichael. *Ghost Ship*'s location work was augmented with filming at Merton Park Studios and Eric Spear, later of *Coronation Street* fame, wrote the film's music.

The Floating Dutchman stars Dermot Walsh as a detective connecting a jewel thief (played by Sidney Tafler) to a body found in the River Thames. *The Floating Dutchman* was an early production of Merton Studios which was based in southwest London, at Merton Park.

Dangerous Voyage was also a Merton Studios production, with a screenplay written by Julia Ward, that Sewell was able to incorporate filming aboard his yacht into. This film is a seafaring thriller that focuses around smuggling on the English Channel. It stars William Lundigan and Naomi Chance. In America the film was released with the alternative title of *Terror Ship*.

At his best, Sewell's storytelling emphasised the power of brevity. He was a director who wasn't interested in connecting characters' flawed and dangerous behaviour to the bigger social picture. He was simply revelling in the pleasures of B-movie storytelling.

A SUMMARY OF PRODUCTION COMPANIES BASED IN WORTHING TODAY

United Magic Studios was established in 2010 by director Jonathan Brooks to produce creative video content for businesses and independent films. Jonathan started United Magic Studios from his bedroom whilst still living with his parents, now they operate from a modern film studio based in Worthing town centre, with an international portfolio of clients. They have produced five short films all of which were filmed in and around Worthing, including a thriller, drama, fantasy, documentary and stop-motion animation.

Future Sun Films was established in 2008 by advertising creative director and film-maker, James Lane. They first began by creating quality online content for clients such as Mercedes-Benz, De Beers and the airline bmi. Future Sun Films now bring many years of international production experience to bear on all manner of commercials, dramas, promos, documentaries and web-series. Establishing firm roots amongst the local film community has created

Filming by Foundlight on Worthing Beach for the trailer for Worthing WOW 2016. (Photo courtesy of the director, Melody Bridges)

working relationships with writers, directors and a large network of actors and crew. The comedy web series *Making Beach* (makingbeach.com) brings conventional, episodic sit-com to a web-savvy audience; evolving storylines, character portraits, one-off scenes all deepen the viewer's experience.

Foundlight was set up by talented film-maker Alan Stockdale who moved to Worthing in 2014. His short film *The Sea and Me* won an award at the South Shorts Film Festival (part of the Worthing WOW festival 2014) and brought his work to the attention of local organisations. Along with creating successful commercials and corporate projects both nationally and internationally, Foundlight worked with the Worthing WOW team to create the festival trailer for the WOW festival in 2015 (celebrating Jane Austen) and 2016 (celebrating the history of film).

SUSSEX FILM OFFICE

And what about film-making in Worthing and Shoreham in the future?

Unlike some other areas in East Sussex such as Hastings and Brighton, which actively pursue film-making in their region, West Sussex has been a little reticent at putting itself forward to encourage film-makers to shoot there. There are some exceptions: Arundel Castle, Petworth House, Weald and Downland Museum and the Witterings have been spotted in film and TV recently. But what of the extraordinary rich and varied landscape and architectural delights West (and East) Sussex has to offer?

In March 2016 Kelly Mikulla launched the Sussex Film Office with the sole purpose of bringing film production to the region. In the first five months of operation the Sussex Film Office worked with forty producers to bring production to the region, including music videos, commercials, corporate videos, photo shoots, TV programmes and films. In September 2016 low-budget British sci-fi film *The Last Boy*, starring Luke Goss and directed by Perry Bhandal, used a variety of locations in Sussex, including Findon, Sompting and Lancing.

For latest news of filming in Sussex or to find out how you could get involved follow Sussex Film Office on Facebook or Twitter.

12

SASE'S SHOREHAM & WORTHING COLLECTIONS

BY FRANK GRAY

Screen Archive South East (SASE), at the University of Brighton and the West Sussex Record Office, serves as the public sector screen archive for the south-east of England. At SASE, we collect, preserve, research and provide access to screen heritage either made in or related to the south-east of England from the nineteenth century to the present. We use the collective noun 'screen' to signify the long history of screen practices and the related screen technologies and screen cultures. Our collection includes a range of screen technologies: the magic lantern from the nineteenth century (hand-drawn, lithographic, photographic), film, video and born digital.

Our Shoreham and Worthing collections represent the different uses of the moving image from the commercial to the amateur. The earliest works are associated with the work of the Progress Film Company on Shoreham Beach from 1919 to 1922. Following on from Sussex's first film studios in Hove (est. 1897), Progress made works of fiction drawn from Victorian and contemporary works of British literature. SASE's two films – *Little Dorrit* (1920) and *The Mayor of Casterbridge* (1921) – are both short versions of the originals but they give a good sense of how Progress and its producer Sidney Morgan possessed an approach that was both faithful to the novels and stylistically conservative. Progress' studio complex was unique at the time given that it comprised a studio, darkroom facilities, a preview theatre and accommodation for cast and crew. It mirrored the new Hollywood studios, albeit on a smaller scale. Progress produced seventeen features for the British market between 1919 and 1922 and this work is very much part of that history of British film and television drama which is associated with national identity and heritage.

ELECTRIC PICTURES

Two SASE amateur collections convey the ways in which film-makers have engaged not with storytelling but with different aspects of community life. Eric Sparks was a Worthing builder and in the late 1930s he made films of everyday scenes in West Sussex with a great emphasis on the railways, especially the new electric lines and the contrasting steam locomotives that connected Sussex with the rest of the country. *Southern Railway* (1937–38), which is both black and white and colour, provides a vivid record of this moment and is distinctive because of the permission Sparks was granted by the Southern Railways Company to film not just at the stations and on the platforms but by the tracks and sheds. It captures the nature of the local economy by representing the railway industry and its role in transporting both passengers and locally grown fruit and vegetables. Paul Plumb was a similar film chronicler. His *A River Runs Through Our Town* (1962) is his 90-minute portrait of Shoreham. Like Sparks' work, this film functions as a moving image time capsule. Here are all aspects of town life including work in the harbour, a Rotary Club lunch, classes at King's Manor School, the presence of post-war pre-fabricated housing, the X-Ray department at Southlands Hospital, football in Buckingham Park, Morris dancing and wreath laying on Remembrance Day. Together Sparks and Plumb demonstrate the value of non-fiction film-making to our understanding of Sussex in the twentieth century and its economic and social history.

SASE continues to collect amateur and professional moving images and is especially interested in working with film-makers who are interested in making new work on all aspects of life in this century.

13

ERIC SPARKS: WORTHING'S SAVIOUR OF SILENT FILM

BY KEVIN BROWNLOW

I have been a film collector since I got my first projector at the age of 11, in 1949. I quickly discovered that many films from the silent film period had been destroyed, and those remaining were being neglected. I was determined to track down as many Hollywood and Continental films from the silent period as I could.

In 1959, I arranged to meet a collector called Eric Sparks at Victoria Station. He lived in Worthing and we had a very interesting talk. He was a builder and decorator in his forties, and evidently had had enough money when he was young to collect films, not 8mm or 9.5mm but 16mm tinted prints, bought direct from America, when they were first issued.

Sparks was a veteran of the Desert Campaign, and said he had fought his way to Cairo, found a Kodascope Library in the town, emptied what he could spare from his kitbag and stuffed in an amber print of *The Grand Duchess and Waiter* (1926). He told me some of his other treasures, and I was astonished to learn that he had an original print of a long-lost Clarence Brown film called *The Signal Tower* (1924). No, he did not want to sell or even exchange this. He was a railway enthusiast and *The Signal Tower* was his favourite railway film.

The film he would be willing to sell was *The Eagle of the Sea* (1926), a historical drama, which sounded very promising. However, he wanted £20 for the five-reeler, twice as much per reel as I was accustomed to paying. I took it home and found it to be a dud. I expressed my regrets to Eric Sparks and as I handed it back, sensed a gulf opening between us.

I tried to repair our relationship, but clearly I was not to be trusted. Over the years I tried to re-establish contact, but to no avail.

In 1965, I was able to meet Clarence Brown in Paris and showed him a couple of his films and he said, 'I didn't know I was that good!' When I realised that he was coming to London, I thought of Mr Sparks and *The Signal Tower*. I rang him up and asked him if he would show the film to the man who made it. I thought he'd be thrilled. He turned me down so bluntly that I lost my temper – and all hope of getting *The Signal Tower*.

I tried once again to make up for my stupidity. Over the years I wrote asking if he would sell it, offering substantial amounts. No response. Then in the mid 1970s, I began working on a television series about the silent era in America called *Hollywood*. Along with the series came film researchers. *The Signal Tower* suddenly became important to the series.

To R.F., our chief film researcher, I typed a memo to ask her to go down to Worthing and try to get Eric Sparks' co-operation. If she couldn't bring him round with her charm, then no one could. I told her, 'You have somehow got to get that *Signal Tower* – just on loan – just long enough to try to get it copied. What an assignment! Worse than being parachuted into France during the war. But much more rewarding if you win!' There was no hope of that. Sparks remained as intransigent as ever.

I had tried everything I could think of, but nothing would elicit a reply, let alone a yes or a no. So with nothing to lose I decided to put another film researcher, R.M., on the spot. R.M. came back from Worthing in a terrible state. It had been pouring with rain, Sparks wouldn't open his door and poor R.M. walked up and down in the downpour till he gave up.

And so it had to be me. I went to Worthing to see Eric Sparks. As I made my way to an ordinary semi-detached house in Chesswood Road, I half-expected it to be fortified. I knocked. A slight noise indicated there was someone there, what was the slight noise? It sounded suspiciously like a bolt being slipped. A very long wait. Eventually, the sound of a great many locks being drawn back and a sleepy character appeared, casually dressed. It was clearly Eric Sparks, twenty years older – long face, not unsympathetic, large nose, the beginning of mutton-chop whiskers. He blinked at me.

'Mr Sparks, we knew each other a long time ago – you don't recognise me.'

He didn't.

'It's Kevin Brownlow.'

'Oh. Kevin Brownlow,' he said, with the resignation of a man being visited by someone about the drains. He reluctantly invited me in. I said we'd last met twenty years ago. What had I done or said that had upset him?

'I really can't say, Mr Brownlow.' He spoke like the manager of a shop to a complaining dowager.

'There must have been something.'

'I suppose it was temperament of some sort.'

I said I'd very much appreciate the chance of talking to him about his early collecting career.

He was clearly an enthusiast and I was a dutiful listener, and while I made no attempts to leap on his films and whisk them away, at least I had made contact.

I invited him to visit me in London.

Eric Sparks came round. He loved railways and silent films. And I had a railway silent he had never seen, *The Westbound Limited*, which he liked a lot. He obviously enjoyed coming to my place. He even gave my small daughter a vast teddy bear, which she named Eric.

Der Tag! A great day – down to Worthing to see *The Signal Tower*. The return to Eric Sparks was surprisingly enjoyable. The last time he had shown it was marked on a label in the can: 1967. It was stupid of me not to have shipped Clarence Brown down there. But it was worth waiting for. Tinted and toned in several colours, beautifully shot in the mountains of Northern California, it was the exciting story of a signalman (Rockliffe Fellowes) whose wife (Virginia Valli) takes in a lodger (Wallace Beery). One stormy night the lodger makes a dead set for the wife, while the signalman struggles to avert a collision between a passenger and a freight train. I just wrote 'A knockout' at the end of my notes.

A month later, Eric Sparks came up from Worthing. We spoke about *Signal Tower*, and he said, 'I tell you what. I'll leave it to you in my will.'

He had been a little off-colour, he told me, but he soon got better. And better. And it was several years before I received a phone call from his solicitors, in 1995.

'Mr Sparks has left you his films,' they said, 'And requested you to remove them all.'

And thus came the day I had so often thought about. My business partner, Patrick Stanbury, drove me to Worthing. A mutual friend was there from the local cine society with a ladder. He said there were so many films — there were even films in the loft. I thought Eric Sparks had just about a dozen features. But every

Kevin Brownlow at Worthing WOW celebrating the Silent Cinema event in 2016. (Julie Edwards)

time we opened a cupboard or chest, films were stacked inside. We found *The Signal Tower* and a few other silents, but the vast majority were episodes from long-forgotten American television series. Hundreds of them. It was like *The Sorcerer's Apprentice*. There were far too many for one trip, and since we had to empty the place of film, we filled Patrick's car and drove to a storage depot in Twickenham. There we had to hire a van and return to Worthing, loading it to the roof. (We inadvertently left a few TV episodes behind.) We drove back to Twickenham to empty the contents and return the van.

We held a party to show *The Signal Tower*. Neil Brand improvised a terrific piano score and although there was one breakdown, it was extremely exciting. As we drank champagne, we toasted Eric Sparks of Worthing for reuniting the world with such a cracker of a film.

PART 2

ELECTRIFYING THE IMAGINATION: CINEMA-GOING IN WORTHING AND SHOREHAM

Worthing and Shoreham's rich cinema-going history mirrors the history of British film exhibition. This section offers an overview of the cinematic landscape of this part of the south coast through the buildings that for 120 years have kept cinema audiences entertained and some of the key players who have helped and still help to make this happen.

14

CINEMA-GOING:
A HISTORY

On 31 August 1896 audiences expecting a typical night of traditional music hall entertainment at the Pier Pavilion, Worthing, were in for a big surprise.

For that week's booking, showman Lt Walter Cole was bringing something special: 'The new wonder – electric animated pictures'. These electric animated pictures had become all the rage in London and other key cities over the past few months, and now they were reaching some of the smaller towns. Films had been seen in the nearby resort of Brighton since March 1896, but it was Lt Cole who brought them in across the border to West Sussex for the first time. In doing so, Cole was following the example of producers in the UK, France and America who were committing themselves to working with the new kind of entertainment.

Although film-makers such as the Lumiere brothers (France), Thomas Edison (USA), Birt Acres (UK) and R.W. Paul (UK) had been making short films throughout 1895, it wasn't until December 1895 that paying audiences began to see these films, when the Lumieres showed a compilation of their films on 28 December 1895 at the Salon Indien in Paris (although some would argue that Edison beat them to it by seven months – see pages 16–18, Dickson in Worthing).

On 21 February 1896 the Lumieres showed their selection of films in London, and, perhaps unsurprisingly, audiences were wowed. Within a month British film pioneer R.W. Paul began screening his films regularly in London. Paul's system for projecting films was known as 'the Theatrograph' and unlike the Lumieres and Edison, who were protective of their equipment and films, Paul was keen to exploit this new medium and work with others to get his films seen.

One of those at the forefront of this new medium was Lt Walter Cole, an internationally renowned ventriloquist who had been headlining in music halls for decades. According to his obituary in *The Gazette* (12 February 1932), he 'held the remarkable distinction of being the first man to tour the country with the cinematograph'.

AND STILL THEY COME.

There appears to be no end to the varieties of projecting apparatus that are being placed on the market. Here is a list of a few which are already being exhibited at the various music halls and places of public entertainment:—The motograph, the animatoscope, the theatrograph, the kinematograph, the projectoscope, the cinemetoscope, the vitascope, the cinematograph, the veriscope, the animatograph, the viveoscope, the eidoloscope, the cinagraphoscope, the biograph, the rayoscope, the magniscope.

Early cinema: an article in the *South Wales Daily News*, 24 July 1897. (The British Library Board)

The *Worthing Gazette*'s review the following week noted: 'the most novel item of the evening's entertainment is the series of animated photos, the newest and most striking electric invention.' And so, cinema had arrived in West Sussex. (More about Lt Walter Cole pp.110–111.)

In these early years, there was an extraordinary range of systems for projecting films as the *South Wales Daily News* (24 July 1897) reported.

However, Worthing residents and visitors were keen to see films more regularly, and in 1906 Michael W. Shanly, who had the deckchair concession in Worthing, amongst other coastal resorts, opened Worthing's first full-time cinema when he converted the Congregational Chapel on the corner of Portland Road and Montague Street. Winter Hall had been in use as an entertainment venue since 1903, but in 1906 it showed films exclusively and became known as Shanly's Cinema (1906–23). The auditorium held 600 and was open daily from 2.30 p.m. to 10.30 p.m. showing films of all genres, with a variety show as part of the programme. It would continue showing films until October 1923, when competition from purpose-built cinemas forced it to close.

In 1908 the Worthing Tabernacle on Montague Street was converted to a mixed purpose entertainment venue including films. Slightly smaller than Shanly's, St James Hall (1908–1925) had a capacity of 500 and held variety shows, concerts as well as film screenings. Mr J.W. Mansfield, who was co-lessee with a Mr Scott, managed it. The *Worthing Herald* (10 February 1956) reported that, 'Mr Mansfield sometimes played his cello in the interval' (Eyre, Gray, Readman, 1995:191). By the early 1920s, films had become only a small percentage of the activity there, and by the mid 1920s St James Hall closed down and became a music shop.

Montague Street, Worthing, *c.* 1916. Shops line each side of the road: on the left is a shop advertising a sale on blouses; further along is St James's Hall Cinema, and on the right is a tobacconist. Clarke's Stores can be seen at the end of the street advertising that it sells ham and bacon as well as being a wine, spirit and beer merchant. (West Sussex Past)

1909–1913

In 1909 the British Parliament introduced the first piece of legislation relating to the film industry. Under the Cinematograph Act of 1909, which was put into effect in January 1910, cinema premises had to adhere to strict safety requirements. Prior to this, films were projected on nitrate film stock that was highly inflammable and there had been a number of fires in the makeshift venues films were being screened in. A key element of this new Act was that all film exhibitors had to house the projector in a fire-resistant projection booth. This legislation greatly encouraged the spread of purpose-built picture houses. One of the first on the south coast was the Duke of York's in Brighton, which was built in 1910, and remains one of the country's least altered cinemas from this period. However, it would be a few more years before Worthing or Shoreham had its own bespoke cinema.

Winton's Hall (1910–27), Shoreham's first cinema, would have had to conform to these regulations. William Edward Winton, a printer in the town, had converted the former Congregational Church of the Countess of Huntingdon's Connexion on Church Street (now Star Lane) into a lecture and concert hall venue in 1908. On 28 February 1910 he was granted a cinematograph licence. Winton continued to run the hall until July 1914 when Arthur Hodgins took over, and renamed it the Star Theatre. Changing hands in 1922 it was operated by Matthews, Holder & Co.

with W.G. Holder taking on the role of manager. In 1924 it was renamed the Court Kinema. On 22 February 1926 the licence was taken over by Frederick Beecham. It closed the following year, returning to its prior use as a chapel. It is currently used by the Co-op for storage.

In 1911 three new cinemas opened, one in Shoreham and two in Worthing.

In June 1911 a garage, built largely of wood, on the High Street, behind the old shipyard, was converted to cinema use. With a corrugated-iron roof and an earth floor, the Bijou Electric Empire (1911–31) initially screened films six days a week. In October 1914 an amendment to its licence allowed Sunday screenings. The year 1914 also saw the start of film production at Shoreham Fort, before moving the following year to a site further down the beach near the Church of the Good Shepherd. Until the studio complex had its own screening facilities, rushes were viewed at the Bijou.

The Shoreham Society collated reminiscences of the locals for the 1994 publication *Memories of Shoreham* (Eyre, Gray, Readman, 1995:184–5). These included visitors to the Bijou who recalled that on rainy days the film's music accompaniment was drowned out by the noise from the corrugated-iron roof. By 1925 it was managed by L.E. Lacroix on behalf of Sussex Picturedrome who also operated the Duke of York's Cinema in Brighton and the Bijou was renamed Duke of York's too. In 1929 the company bought the freehold and the following year sold it to E.R. Sutter who owned a nearby yacht-building yard, who in turn leased it to A.B. Chipper.

The Star Cinema, then and now. (Courtesy of Roger Bateman)

The Bijou Cinema in Shoreham High Street. (Courtesy of Roger Bateman)

On Wednesday 5 August 1931 the Duke of York's caught fire and was completely destroyed.

During 1911 the roller skating rink on Gratwicke Road in Worthing was converted into the Cinema Elite (1911–15). Manager B.R. Stent had an aggressive admission price policy, undercutting its competition. This may well have been a contributing factor to its place in Worthing's cinema history, which was short lived, as it closed in 1915.

Worthing's longest serving building for exhibiting films is the Worthing Dome (1911–present), which was originally part of the Kursaal, the brainchild of Swiss impresario Carl Adolf Seebold. Seebold began working on his complex of entertainment venues in June 1910, and by October the following year this had developed into a magnificent multi-purpose venue, which featured the town's first purpose-built cinema: The Electric Palace. Its Coronation Hall was used for roller skating, concerts and meetings and the whole property was surrounded by extensive gardens.

The films Seebold showed in the Electric Theatre (mainly silent animations) were so popular that in 1913 he converted the Coronation Hall into a second cinema. It was renamed the Dome in 1915. In 1918 he began a redevelopment programme to make these changes permanent and in 1921 it reopened as a cinema and ballroom. In the 1920s Seebold acquired two further cinemas in Worthing, the Rivoli and the Picturedrome. After the Second World War the cinema fell into disrepair, and in 1955, a few years after his death in 1951, the new owners hired architects Goldsmith and Pennells to install a new cinemascope screen.

In 1969, Worthing Borough Council purchased the freehold of the Dome specifically to redevelop the area. The ensuing thirty years proved to be turbulent, with the ownership being transferred between private companies and the council. The state of the building deteriorated further and at periods had to be closed for safety

The Kursaal at night. A photographic postcard probably of the opening of the building, which was built in 1910. (West Sussex Past)

Worthing Dome, screen one. (Photograph by Gary Levett)

reasons. On 9 November 1999 the Worthing Dome & Regeneration Trust paid the council a nominal fee of £10 and took possession of the cinema.

The Dome Cinema reopened its doors in July 2007 after a two-year closure to undergo a £2.3 million makeover. This was made possible with a Heritage Lottery Fund grant of £1.6 million being awarded to the Worthing Dome and Regeneration Trust. English Heritage also endorsed the project by contributing £200,000.

Both the Worthing Dome and the adjacent bus depot appear prominently in *Wish You Were Here* (1987); Eric (Tom Bell) plays the cinema's projectionist.

1914–1928

The most recent addition to Worthing's roster was the Picturedrome (1914–present, but not always as a cinema), which opened in July 1914. In 1916 the Connaught Hall was built adjacent to it for dances, concerts and drama performances. The 1921 makeover at the Dome and the arrival of the new, much smarter, Rivoli Cinema in 1924 saw the Picturedrome fall down the pecking order and it became harder and harder for them to get the latest big releases. In 1926 Seebold took it on, managing it alongside the Rivoli and Dome and within a few years with the arrival of sound, all three cinemas were converted for talkies, but times were tough with newer cinemas opening. In 1935 Seebold spent £60,000 adding a new art deco facade, building a fly tower and putting in a stage where the screen had been and, in the reverse of many cinemas which were being converted from theatres, a cinema became a theatre.

The Connaught today. (Courtesy of the Worthing Theatres)

The Worthing Repertory Company which had outgrown the Connaught Hall took over the Picturedrome, renamed the New Connaught Theatre. The Connaught Hall remained unused until 1940 after an application to turn it into a cinema had been turned down in 1936. From 1940 to 1945 it was used as a theatre, and in 1945 it was converted into the Ritz ballroom, in use until 1950, after which it was used as a rehearsal space and scenery painting studio for the theatre. The Connaught closed for a period in 1966 and was taken over by Worthing Borough Council in 1967. It was forced to close in 1980–81 and then again in 1983. The venue closed in January 1986, its future looking very grim. Local residents, the Wilson brothers, caught the public's attention and created national headlines with their efforts to keep the Connaught open (see pp. 113–114). It reopened in February 1987 following a transfer in ownership to Worthing Borough Council and underwent a £250,000 face-lift. The Connaught Theatre offered a mixed programme of live performance and film; the first film screened there was *A Chorus Line* on Monday 2 March. In June 1995 the former Ritz ballroom was restored and reopened with the Jodie Foster film *Nell*. Since then, it has been a dual-use cinema/theatre with both auditoria having facilities for screening films.

By 1914 permanent purpose-built cinemas were to be found in virtually every town. The outbreak of the war saw a temporary cessation in many building projects. However, in Shoreham, the emergence of the army camp saw the YMCA and Salvation Army developing relaxation spaces for soldiers. This included a cinema tent that was in use until 1916. As part of the camp a cheaply built garrison theatre with fly tower on New Road was built, which in 1920 became the Coliseum Theatre (1920–41), a dual theatre-cinema.

The Connaught in March 1950. (Courtesy of the Worthing Theatres)

The Connaught auditorium in 1950. (Courtesy of the Worthing Theatres)

The Connaught foyer and box office in 1950. (Courtesy of the Worthing Theatres)

Initially owned by M.J.H. Browne and managed by Queenie Millard, ticket prices at the Coliseum were slightly higher than those at the Star. It was unusual for a town the size of Shoreham to have so many theatres, but given the studio complex on the beach, interest in the films was high and this promoted healthy competition between the three cinemas. In 1923 the Coliseum was taken over by the Blue Flash Cinema Company, a company founded by former officers of the 4th Battalion of the Royal Sussex Regiment. The company's policy was to employ as many of the regiment's demobilised personnel as possible. They ran the Coliseum in conjunction with the Capitol in Horsham, which they had built the same year. Both venues showed live theatre and film, employing a rear projection system from the back of the stage for film screenings. It changed hands in 1925 and 1930. In 1935 Frederick John Freeman, who had opened the Norfolk Cinema in 1933, took control of the Collie (as it was colloquially known). The following year both cinemas were in the hands of Louis Halpern, who continued operating both until 1941 when the increasing difficulties of wartime travel forced him to close the Coliseum and to focus on the Norfolk. The building was used as a machine shop until the 1960s. It was later demolished, and the site is now occupied by council offices.

The Coliseum Cinema, Shoreham. (By kind permission of Marlipins Museum, Sussex Archaeological Society)

Many cinemas had suffered during the First World War, but as cinema construction resumed, vast new super cinemas began to appear in major cities. The now demolished Regent at Brighton, built in 1921, seated 2,200 and featured a restaurant, café, tearoom and ballroom above the auditorium. It would be three years until Worthing got its own super cinema. Having successfully transformed the Kursaal into the Dome Cinema, Seebold sought to extend his cinema empire by building, in 1924, Worthing's first big cinema, the Rivoli (1924–60) on Chapel Road on the junction with North Street. At a cost of £75,000 (£4.1 million today) the Rivoli held 1,680 people in two tiers and boxes. It had a pipe organ, an eleven-piece orchestra, a sliding roof and large tearooms. It opened on 10 March 1924 with Douglas Fairbanks' *Robin Hood*. In 1929 Worthing audiences would witness their first talking movie, *The Singing Fool* starring Al Jolson. Given its opulence and size it remained competitive with the newer Odeon and Plaza cinemas until 1959 when Odeon's relationship with Rank meant that Rivoli was getting an inferior range of films. On the morning of 19 January 1960 two policemen spotted smoke coming from the cinema. Nearly seventy firemen fought the blaze but to no avail, the roof collapsed and the auditorium was gutted. Seebold's widow decided against rebuilding. The cinema's facade was retained until it was demolished in 1984 as part of the Chapel Road widening scheme.

1928–1934

When the part-talkie *The Jazz Singer* (1927) opened in London in September 1928 only one cinema (the Piccadilly on Denman Street) had been equipped to accommodate it. Worthing would have to wait until Al Jolson's next film *The Singing Fool* to hear what all the fuss was about.

The arrival of sound films was a major financial outlay for cinemas across the globe, and over the coming months all Worthing and Shoreham's cinemas would make the transition.

In 1933 both Shoreham and Worthing saw new cinemas being built. On 27 March 1933 the Norfolk (1933–64), renamed the Ritz in 1947, opened on Norfolk Bridge, Victoria Road, Shoreham. With 700 seats it was smaller than the recent super cinemas and it was all on one level. Recalling the cinema for *Memories of Shoreham*, the opinions vary from 'the great centre for us young people' to 'a building of no interest', 'dismal cinema', 'a very basic cinema' and 'very shabby and of poor construction'. Despite its poor construction it went through various managements, surviving (just) through the period of widescreen spectacles that it couldn't accommodate. It struggled on into the 1960s but in 1963 it became a shared-usage venue with bingo, until 1964 when closed. It was demolished in the 1970s.

Norfolk Cinema on Old Shoreham Road. (Courtesy of Roger Bateman)

Possibly one of the reasons why locals were so dismissive of the Norfolk was that in December 1933 Worthing saw the arrival of the Plaza (1933–68) on Rowlands Road. With an impressive 2,005 seats the Plaza was the largest cinema in West Sussex, and was the first cinema in Worthing with a full air-conditioning system (the Rivoli relying on its sliding roof to get fresh air on warm evenings). Work began on the Plaza Cinema on the corner of Rowlands Road and Eriswell Road in December 1932 by noted cinema architect Harry Weston. Described as a 'super cinema' it cost £80,000 (now £5 million) and opened on 14 December 1933 with the Bebe Daniels film *The Song You Gave Me*. It was built by Lou Morris who had a reputation for building cinemas and selling them off quickly at a profit, and the Plaza was no exception.

In 1934 Seebold agreed to take on the Plaza that would have given him the monopoly on Worthing cinemas. Morris accepted Seebold's deposit but then sold the shares to the cinema's architect Harry Weston. When it emerged that Weston was representing Odeon's interest, Seebold sued Morris and received a small settlement. Meanwhile Odeon had plans to build their own cinema, and leased the Plaza to Associated British Cinemas (ABC), a national chain. The Plaza remained in ABC's network until it closed its doors in December 1968, the last film screened there was the Shirley MacLaine movie *The Bliss of Mrs Blossom*. The cinema reopened as a bingo hall in January 1969. In 1970 the organ was removed and was installed in an electronics works near Perth, Western Australia. The stalls area remains in use as a bingo hall run by Gala Bingo, the upper levels are used for storage. (Former projectionist Brian Meetens shares his memories of the Plaza pp.111–112).

In a few short years Oscar Deutsch, founder of the Odeon chain, had quickly established himself as the behemoth of British cinemas. He began planning his domination of film exhibition in 1931, and when the Worthing Odeon (1934–87) opened in Liverpool Gardens on 24 March 1934 he had already eight cinemas in his chain (at its peak it would have 300), including the nearby Lancing Odeon. At this point, many were fairly undistinguished (the sleek art deco style not established by this point across all acquisitions and new builds) but not the Worthing Odeon, which was considered a landmark in British cinema architecture when it opened. The Odeon had 1,531 seats over two levels. It cost £32,500 to build (now £2.1 million) with furnishings and equipment coming in at another £6,000 (£387,000). Given its seaside location and other cinema competition in town this Odeon, unlike the majority of the chain, incorporated a café and organ.

It remained relatively unchanged for almost thirty years. In 1962 the organ was removed and in 1964 a new restaurant was created over two floors. After forty years

A 1952 advert for Worthing Plaza. (Courtesy of Roger Bateman)

Odeon Cinema and Liverpool Terrace Gardens, Worthing, *c*. 1944. View from Liverpool Road (right) into Liverpool Gardens. On the left, there is a bicycle propped against the kerb and a man walking past a sign that reads 'Public Air Raid Shelter'. On the right is a handcart with a poster advertising the 1944 film *It Happened Tomorrow*, starring Dick Powell, Linda Darnell and Jack Oakie. (Walter Gardiner Photography Collection, West Sussex Past)

as a single-screen cinema in 1984 it was converted into a three-screener at a cost of £70,000 (£764,000): the largest screen seating 450 and two smaller screens with 120 seats each. Ten years later, with cinema admissions across the UK plummeting, the building was sold to property developers in 1984, and Odeon continuing to operate it for a further two years, it closed on 27 September 1986. Local opposition to this demolition led to English Heritage listing it in spring 1987. The developers, a tad miffed by this, arranged to have a structural survey and found that the tower and upper part of the facade were dangerous and permission was granted for it to be demolished, which it was. The site was redeveloped as part of a shopping and office complex.

1934–2012

And so, 1934 saw the last purpose-built cinema being constructed in Worthing. Despite audiences being at their peak following the end of the Second World War, the construction of new cinemas was effectively ended.

In 1946 cinema-going in Britain was at its highest with a record 1.64 billion tickets sold. But times were a-changing; in 1945 it was reported that there were only 15,000 television sets in Britain, by 1955, when commercial television started, there

The Odeon Cinema, Worthing, in February 1988 after demolition work had begun. Photograph by Mrs N.F. Coviello. (West Sussex Past)

were 5 million and by 1961 there were 11 million sets and in the same period cinema admissions had fallen by 75 per cent. By the 1960s the grand cinemas that had been built thirty to forty years earlier were falling into disrepair and were closing. By the end of the 1960s all Shoreham's cinemas were closed – the last one standing was the Norfolk which had closed in 1964, and Worthing lost two, the Rivoli in 1960 and the Plaza in 1968.

By 1970 UK cinema attendance had dropped to 193 million admissions, by 1980 down to 110 million, and in 1984, when the Odeon was converted from three to one screen, annual cinema admissions were at an all time low of 54 million. This was in part due to the rise of wider television choice and the growth of VHS. But there was a small glimmer of hope for film distributors, a new kind of cinema-going experience was on the horizon: the Multiplex. In 1985 the first multiplex cinema was built in Milton Keynes and soon began to open across the UK. The multiplex cinemas are largely devoid of architectural charm, and are effectively large warehouses with multiple screens. UK film-makers and exhibitors initially envisaged a period of cinema utopia. With so many screens available surely there would be a regular screen reserved for British or foreign films? And now, 60 per cent of UK screens are to be in found in multiplexes, who rely as much on food and beverage sales as they do on cinema ticket sales, and their screens are dominated by Hollywood products.

The last films shown at the Odeon Worthing in 1987 were, in screen one, the US sci-fi sequel *Aliens* and on screen two, the low-budget British films *Letter to Brezhnev* and *My Beautiful Launderette*. Another Hollywood picture played in Screen Three, *FX: Murder by Illusion*.

2012–2016

The format of varied programming is one that the BFI are keen to restore, which is why, in 2012 the BFI launched its five-year Film Forever strategy. Aware that its resources are a relatively modest part of the overall film finance landscape, it determined to focus on three priority areas only: expanding education and learning, and boosting audience choice; supporting the future success of British film; and unlocking our film heritage.

Within this strategy, funding was made available through the BFI Film Audience Network to support film festivals and to launch a number of regional film hubs to encourage cinema exhibitors to programme specialist film content, which would include independent, foreign-language, archive and classic films.

The latest figures (2015) for UK-wide cinema attendance show annual admissions reaching 71.9 million, 9 per cent up on the previous years. Currently, Worthing has two thriving full-time cinemas: the Worthing Dome and the Connaught. The Worthing Film Club, founded in 2007, meets monthly at the Connaught to screen innovative and compelling films from around the world. Shoreham has no full-time cinemas but its mixed-use arts centre, the Ropetackle, is home to Film at Ropetackle (formerly Shoreham Film Club). Founded in 2011, its initial programme of screening ten films a year has expanded, and it now offers a wider range of films to its core members and those that require special screening conditions. On most Thursdays at West Street Lofts in Shoreham you can partake in one of their film and food nights.

Looking Ahead

At the time of writing (summer 2016) there are two on-going activities that may once again signal a shift in Worthing and Shoreham's cinema landscape.

The *Worthing Herald* ran a news story on 14 July 2016 under the heading 'Union Place deal to boost hopes of multiplex cinema' in which it outlined concern that, 'The plan could, however, negatively affect the adjacent Connaught Theatre which generates more than £300,000 from its cinema operation annually.' Director for the Economy for Worthing Borough Council, Martin Randall, is quoted as saying that there 'would be an impact' and that the (Connaught) cinema would 'have to adapt'. The multiplex is part of a £3 million deal that the council hopes to strike with developers for a mixed-use site incorporating new homes, restaurants and a six-screen cinema. However, this is not the first time the council has tried to redevelop the site, with similar news stories running in 2010 and 2014. We wait to see!

The BFI's optimistically titled 2012 strategy BFI Film Forever will be drawing to an end in 2017. In summer 2016 the BFI were in consultation with relevant organisations and cinemagoers to assess the success of its initial priorities and structures. The current funding for the regional Films Hubs ends in March 2017. Worthing and Shoreham falls under Film Hub South East, which takes in all cinema exhibitions in Kent, Surrey, East and West Sussex, Isle of Wight, Hampshire, Berkshire and Oxfordshire. The Worthing Connaught, Worthing WOW and Ropetackle Film Society have all been recipients of grant applications to support themed film seasons. Here's hoping that their findings will continue to fund and support innovative film programming across the country.

LT WALTER COLE (1844–1932)
BY ELLEN CHESHIRE

On 31 August 1896 Lt Walter Cole and his touring variety show started a one-week engagement at the Worthing Pier Pavilion. As part of his line-up he, for the first time, incorporated the latest wonder of the age 'Electric Animated Photos'.

Two weeks earlier, at his engagement in nearby Brighton, films were not featured as part of his press announcements.

Walter Cole had been touring since 1869 with his ventriloquism act. He was famous for performing with life-size dolls, known as The Merry Folks, and was considered an expert at both near- and far-distance work. His obituary in *The Era*, the UK's leading theatrical newspaper of the time, reported that, 'he was the first man to introduce to English audiences life-size figures, and he was able to carry on a conversation between five or six dolls at the same time.'

He was a consummate showman, touring with his own variety show entitled *Two Hours of Refined Mirth with Lieut. Walter Cole, the Highly Gifted and Popular Ventriloquist* and appearing on the bill of major music hall theatres with some of the leading performers the day. He appeared by command of HRH Prince of Wales at Marlbough House, London, and Prince Henry of Lichtenstein and before various Lord Mayors of London at Mansion House.

Punch magazine exclaimed 'Lieutenant COLE; Why, he is far above that rank; he is King COLE, King of Ventriloquists, with an exhibition of cleverness that no COLE, who has ever had anything to do with any sort of exhibition, has ever equalled. He is the only COLE that might be sent successfully to Newcastle.' Whilst *The Times* simply stated that he was 'the Greatest Ventriloquist in the world'. This is perhaps why in the *Worthing Gazette*'s review on 2 September 1896 they wrote: '[Cole's] annual visit is recognised as one of the most popular features of the Pier season.' (*Punch* and *The Times* reviews quoted in Cole's publicity material, no dates given)

Audiences were promised 'refined fun', 'ventriloquial surprises', 'new, novel & original comic operettas', 'humourous songs' and 'biloquial wonders'.

So, for audiences at the Pier Pavilion Worthing in August 1896, excitement at seeing Cole and his Merry Folks, and his company of 'first class artistes' would have been high. But it is clear how much of an impact early films had on audiences and critics when the following week the review in the *Worthing Gazette*

(2 September 1896) praised: 'The ventriloquial entertainment is brought well up to date, and Lieut. Cole has the support of a clever company; but the most novel item of the evening's entertainment is the series of animated photos, the newest and most striking electric invention. Lieut. Cole has a very strong attraction in this department of his refreshingly original show.'

Cole had begun practising ventriloquism when he was a young boy growing up, the son of a doctor in the Old Kent Road, mimicking the sounds of the buses' toots. He left school at 18 and began life as a sailor with the Royal Mail Steam Packet Company. He stayed at sea for eight years, refining his ventriloquism skills by entertaining his fellow sailors. His first professional engagement as a ventriloquist was in Manchester where he earned £2 10s per week. He continued to tour outside London for a year, before getting his first London engagement at the Egyptian Hall in the early 1870s, to great acclaim. He toured Europe and wherever he went he performed in their native language. He was crowned 'The king of ventriloquists' and is credited as being the first ventriloquist to throw his voice to the roof of a building. He was acclaimed the 'prince of mirth-makers' for he also entertained audiences with his comic performances as an old Scottish lady, a jolly Lancashire lad and a little girl amongst others.

But it is for use of the cinematograph that we include him here, and his importance in the field of early cinema exhibition is reinforced by the headline of his obituary in *The Gazette* (12 February 1932), which stated that he was the 'World-famous ventriloquist who pioneered the English Cinematograph industry'. The obituary recalls, 'But he did not confine himself to pioneering in one sphere only, he held the remarkable distinction of being the first man to tour the country with the cinematograph', showing the films of R.W. Paul.

He retired from the stage in 1904, coming out of retirement during the First world War to entertain wounded soldiers, and to make appearances at local community events and children's parties. He died in Enfield on Saturday 5 February 1932, aged 87.

WORTHING'S SUPER CINEMA
BY BRIAN MEETENS

In the late 1950s I joined the projection team at the Plaza in Rowlands Road, which had opened twenty-five years earlier on 14 December 1933.

Classified as a 'super cinema' it truly was super! With an auditorium that held 2,000, a stunning art deco facade, a magnificent Compton organ, a ballroom, plus a very large stage and scene dock, the Plaza really was the place to be seen during its heyday in the 1930s, '40s and early '50s.

There was an interesting rumour that the Plaza could well have been called the 'Ocean' and any of you who frequented the building when it was still a cinema may have noticed a number of underwater-themed features that tended to bear this out, including: doors fitted with small round windows resembling portholes; walls plastered into gentle wave shaped textures; the houselights grille high up on the ceiling seemed to be shaped to give an impression of the surface of the sea viewed while swimming underwater; and the screen curtains (or 'tabs' in the business) were patterned with fish.

However, for me, it was the projection room that was the most fascinating aspect of the cinema. Unlike many projection rooms that were completely enclosed, the Plaza's had access, via doors, to the open air, allowing us to look down and view everything going on in the busy street and shops at the western end of Montague Street, while at the same time manually rewinding the reel that had just been shown. It was also considerably larger than most from that era and incorporated two 35mm projectors with 2,000ft-capacity spool-boxes, a spotlight to highlight the ice-cream girls in the interval, a slide projector and a mercury rectifier which converted the AC current to DC for the projectors' carbon-arc lamps.

The Plaza's heyday was the 1940s and early '50, where queues would often stretch from the front doors around the side under the very considerate covered walkway, which protected cinema patrons from the rain and wind. Installed in 1953, the Plaza boasted one of the widest screens in the south: 125ft wide. However, by the time I joined even the newest fad of widescreen films was no match for the comforts of watching television at home.

Cinema audiences generally started to decline and an audience of 400–500 in the Plaza's 2,000-seat auditorium seemed almost lost. Any less and it appeared deserted. The 1960s arrived and apart from a few pop concerts staged in the early part of the decade the Plaza plodded on screening films. With audiences continuing in this downward trend, Worthing's super cinema finally closed its doors in 1968 and became a bingo hall. Despite it no longer being in use as a cinema I'm pleased that the building is still there, a permanent reminder of Worthing's super cinema.

Brian Meetens was a projectionist at the Plaza during the latter part of the 1950s, a member of Shoreham Cine Club from the 1970s and one of the founder members of South Downs Video and Film-makers in 1989. Now known as South Downs Film-makers, this friendly film-making club near Worthing make and screen films across a number of film genres – dramas, comedies, documentaries and animations.
www.southdownsfilmmakers.org.uk

THE WILSON BROTHERS
BY KAREN MCCREEDY

When the phrase 'Dying to go to the theatre' is employed, it's generally in the context of being extremely excited about seeing a particular show. But in the case of the Wilson brothers of Worthing, the phrase almost became a literal one. For in 1986 Roy and Michael Wilson went on hunger strike to save Worthing's Connaught Theatre.

Michael (a film cameraman) and Roy (an actor who appeared in films with Wilfrid Lawson and Dulcie Gray) lived within 300 yards of the Connaught. When it closed on 18 January 1986, they were so distraught that they immediately announced that they would go on hunger strike until there was an undertaking to reopen the theatre. Their stance garnered publicity across the globe, though opinions vary on whether their actions ultimately made a difference.

Over the course of forty-six days, Roy and Michael lost around 2 stone apiece, and Michael almost slipped into a coma. On hearing that the theatre would reopen, he said: 'The first 10 days were the worst ... But it was all worthwhile and we are overjoyed at the news of the Connaught.' (*The Stage*, 27 February 1986)

The Wilson brothers make the cover of *The Stage*, 23 January 1986. (Courtesy of *The Stage*)

113

Away from the media glare, a working party chaired by Tony MacMillan, and advised by theatre consultant Patrick Boyd Maunsell, had shifted the political scenery. It was thanks to their suggestions and recommendation that Worthing Borough Council accepted that the Connaught should reopen on a forty-six-week annual basis, and injected the necessary cash to help reopen it.

In his book *Full Circle: The Story of Worthing's Connaught Theatre*, John Willmer writes that the brothers were 'nothing more than an irrelevant nuisance'. But it was Michael and Roy's exploits that were highlighted in *The Stage* in December 1986 when the theatre reopened (on 13 December 1986) with a 'thanksgiving party' for 150 guests – 'Hunger Strike Victory' the headline read.

Reports that their story was to become the subject of a musical (*The Stage*, 5 October 1986), a TV play (*The Stage*, 22 January 1987) and a stage play (*Evening Argus*, 29 January 1987) came to nothing, and Roy died only three years later aged 55. It was thought that the hunger strike had contributed to his premature death.

Michael died on 26 March 2006, aged 77. His obituary in *The Stage* was almost entirely devoted to his, and his brother's, sacrifices for the cause when they 'forced the council into a dramatic U-Turn after receiving worldwide coverage'.

Karen McCreedy has written articles about British history and films for **Classic Television***,* **Yours***, and* **Best of British** *magazines and for the book* **Under Fire: A Century of War Movies***.*

15

ECHOES OF LANCING'S CINEMAS PAST

BY ELLEN CHESHIRE

L ancing, three and half miles from Worthing and four and a half miles from Shoreham, is according to the Visit Worthing website 'reportedly the largest village in England with a population of over 19,000'. Despite this population there has not been a cinema in Lancing since the Luxor closed in 1965.

Oscar Deutsch opened his first cinema in Dudley in 1928, and quickly built a chain of cinemas across the country. The Lancing Odeon (1933–52) in Penhill Street was opened on 31 October 1933, by which point he had twenty-six cinemas. The Lancing Odeon was the fifth cinema to be built specifically for Odeon and had a capacity of 691. It cost £9,600 (now £603,552) to build, but it was never as successful (or attractive) as the nearby Worthing Odeon (which cost £40,700, now £2.624 million) which opened in March 1934. Seen very much as the 'poor relation', in March 1936 it was renamed the Regal but still run as part of the Odeon circuit until 1939 when it was leased to Basil Fortesque who was building the much grander Luxor in Lancing. Two months after the Luxor opened, Fortesque closed the Regal. It was returned to Odeon in October 1941 who leased it to Mrs I. Merriman-Langdon who was running the Rothbury Cinema in Portslade. But this operation was short-lived. Due to wartime restrictions it became increasingly difficult to operate and encourage visitors, and in August 1942 it was back in Odeon's hands. In March 1945 its name was reverted back to Odeon who continued to operate it until January 1952, when it was sold to Shipman and King (S&K) who were taking over the Luxor, who immediately closed it. The last films shown there included one of the first films in Britain to be given the X-certificate by the British Board of Film Classification (BBFC), the French comedy *Clochemerle* (1948), and British wartime comedy *Appointment with*

Venus (1951). The building is still there, now called Regal House, and its cinematic roots are still very much in evidence.

The Luxor Lancing (1939–65) is probably the more well known due to its prominent location opposite the train station on the aptly name Station Parade. Designed by architect W. Frazer-Granger for Basil Fortesque, it was intended to be dual purpose – hosting both films and live theatre. It was larger than the Odeon, seating 998 on two levels. It opened in January 1940 (with Sydney Samuelson as its rewind boy) with The Crazy Gang in *Frozen Limits* (1939). In 1942 it was taken over by the London-based cinema exhibitors H. Bentley whose other cinemas were predominately in Essex. In the early 1950s it was up for sale again and in 1952 it was bought by S&K, who had also bought the Odeon (which they closed). They also ran the Hailsham Pavilion and a small chain of cinemas in country towns. It continued as a mixed-use theatre and cinema until 1957, from which point it exclusively showed films until June 1965. Its last week-long film screening was David Lean's *Lawrence of Arabia* (1962) which was the first film shot in Panavision to win a Best Cinematography Oscar. And who was responsible for bringing the Panavision cameras to UK? And ensuring that expert support and advice was available twenty-four-seven for cinematographers such as Freddie Young? None other than Samuelson Film Services Ltd, who, through Sir Sydney Samuelson's dogged determination and chutzpah, had acquired the European rights for Panavision.

The Luxor was used as a bingo hall until the 1980s when the auditorium was knocked down for flats. The distinctive facade remains with shops and it was in one of these that a small fire started on 15 August 2016. With three fire engines in attendance the fire was contained. The *Worthing Herald* reported:

> A spokesperson for the fire service confirmed that it was a fire on the ground floor in the derelict part of the building, and that it was extinguished using four breathing apparatus and two jets. They said it was being treated as a 'deliberate ignition', and added that no-one was in the building at the time of the blaze.

This near miss sparked concern with locals and within the month, on 8 September, *Shoreham Herald* reported the encouraging news that, 'The derelict building in South Street has been made an asset of community value (ACV), meaning the community will be involved in any process were it to be put up for sale.'

Did you know?
Despite being one of the most magnificent buildings in Sussex, Lancing College has never been *seen* in a feature film. *Sussex Life Magazine* (April 2014) reported that, 'It was, however, used for the 2008 film version of *Brideshead Revisited*, where the voices of boys chattering and footsteps in the cloisters were recorded for background sounds.'

16

'HOW LUCKY CAN YOU BE!' SIR SYDNEY SAMUELSON CBE

BY ELLEN CHESHIRE

'Sydney really is a mensch or as Nietzsche would say an übermensch, there almost isn't a menschy enough word to use of such a mensch.' Such praise, but as Stephen Fry also said at the British Film and Television Veterans' All Industry Tribute to Sir Sydney Samuelson in 2011: 'If you throw a brick in a town square in middle England it would not be likely to connect with the cranium of a person who knew who Sir Sydney Samuelson was, which is just the way Sydney likes it.'

At this tribute Sir Sydney Samuelson, aged 86, walked on to the stage of London's Grand Connaught Rooms to a standing ovation of British film professionals and accepted a Lifetime Achievement Award for services to the British film industry. But this wasn't the first of such awards he had received. In 1978 he was appointed a Commander of the Order of the British Empire (CBE), in 1985 he was awarded the Michael Balcon Award, in 1993 a Fellowship of BAFTA (the Academy's highest honour), in 1994 he was the surprise 'victim' of ITV's *This is Your Life* (13 April 1994) hosted by Michael Aspel and in 1995, probably the highest honour one can receive, a knighthood.

Sir Sydney has been honoured in this way because as Stephen Fry remarked: 'The fact that there is even a British film industry at all I'm honestly prepared to say is in large part due to the life and work of Sir Sydney.'

So what was Sir Sydney Samuelson's life and work?

Born on 7 December 1925, Sydney was one of four boys born to silent film producer/director G.B. (Bertie) Samuelson (1889–1947) and silent film star mother Marjorie Statler (1901–89). Clearly film was in Sydney's DNA, or as Lord (David) Puttnam puts it, 'British cinema runs through [Sydney] like a stick of rock' (in *All Tribute Souvenir Brochure*).

Bertie had begun making films in 1913 and it is believed that he had made seventy films by 1921. Tastes were beginning to change, and Bertie's output had slowed by the time his children started to arrive in 1924. Marjorie appeared in a number of films including *She* (1925), Leander de Cordova's second adaptation of a H. Rider Haggard novel after *Swallow* (1922) in which Joan Morgan had starred. One of his last films was *The Callbox Murder Mystery* (1932) which had a screenplay by Joan Wentworth Wood (aka Joan Morgan). In 1931 G.B. Samuelson Films had been declared bankrupt, and soon after the family was initially split between the south coast where Sydney and his elder brother David went to Shoreham Grammar School, whilst their father ran a lending library in Worthing and their mother and two younger brothers stayed in Hendon in north-west London. By 1937, with the lending library business failing, the entire family relocated to Lancing, where Marjorie opened a wool shop in Shoreham and the boys left the grammar school for state schools.

It was whilst going to and from school in 1939 that Sydney saw the Luxor Cinema, Lancing, being built, and given that he was to be 14 by the end of the year and eligible to leave school, enquired whether there was any work for a young man with an interest in films. In January 1940 he started his career in film as a 'rewind boy' at the Luxor. The chief projectionist never took to Sydney as he had been hired by the cinema's owner and not himself, and so it was only on the chief's day off that the second projectionist initiated Sydney into the art of cinematic projection. He had been there just over a year when Bertie,

Sydney Samuelson, aged 14. (Courtesy of Sir Sydney Samuelson)

who had been desperate to get a job, any job, was given the thankless task to supervise two film storage depots at Great Barr, near Birmingham. The family relocated and Sydney worked as projectionist in the Birmingham area, before joining the air force, but didn't see action as the war ended.

Stuck at RAF Stanmore on his 21st birthday, in 1946, Sydney attended a film screening of *Pride and Prejudice* (1940). When the film broke Sydney was called in to fix it. This was a great relief to the audience and the expectant crowd were pleased and thankful to Sydney's projections prowess. He certainly caught the attention of one young lady, 18-year-old Doris, whom he married three years later.

Realising that a career in cinema projection might be a little limiting he followed his older brother, David, into film production. Initially working as a cameraman for newsreel production, in 1953 he and his brother David were part of the elite team of cameramen charged with capturing the most anticipated TV event – the Queen's Coronation. When a camera broke down minutes before the event was due to start, it was Sydney's know-how that saved the day.

He then joined the Colonial Film Unit in Africa, and in 1954 after a ten-month period away filming in Nigeria he had saved £300. Initially he and Doris thought to use it as a deposit on a house, but instead used it as a deposit on a Newman Sinclair number 612 camera, which cost £800. He had one year to pay back the remaining £500 before he would start accruing interest. And so Samuelson Film Services Ltd

Evening Standard newsstand with news of Sydney Samuelson's appointment as film commissioner. (Courtesy of Sir Sydney Samuelson)

(Samuelsons) was born as he hired out the camera whenever he wasn't using it. Soon one camera became three, and then an empire.

'Samuelsons' was committed to providing the highest quality equipment and expertise to film and television production in the UK, and were invested in pushing the boundaries of filming equipment to help produce the most amazing film images, including the James Bond movies, *Oliver!* (1968) and *Gandhi* (1982).

But his engagement with the film industry didn't end there. From 1973–76 Sydney was the Chairman of BAFTA and was instrumental in ensuring the new BAFTA HQ at 195 Piccadilly was renovated. He dreamt up innovative fundraising schemes and events, and bent the arm and the ear of pretty much everyone in the British film industry.

In 1991 when Margaret Thatcher was looking for a mover and shaker to be the UK's first film commissioner, she invited Sydney to take up this important role.

The primary function of the newly formed British Film Commission was to encourage Hollywood film companies to film in Britain. And come they did. *Mission: Impossible* (1996), *The Fifth Element* (1997), *Saving Private Ryan* (1998), and *Star Wars* (1999) are among the films Sydney lured to these shores under his six-year tenure.

In 2016, Sir Sydney Samuelson travelled back to Worthing as part of Worthing WOW's celebration of film in Sussex, where he spoke to a crowded room at the Connaught Theatre about his early life in Shoreham, Lancing and Worthing. He still sits on the board of a number of film industry organisations and retains an active interest in aspects of film. Not bad for a man who started his life rewinding reels of 35mm at a cinema in Lancing. But as he himself says, 'How lucky can you be!'

Sir Sydney Samuelson at Worthing WOW, 2016. (Julie Edwards)

17

HERITAGE TRAIL

There's a quiet thrill and a tingle of excitement that might come into focus when you come across a real place that has featured in a movie.

With that tingle factor in mind, we've put together this Electric Pictures Movie Heritage Trail: taking in both film locations and also notable local cinema sites.

As part of Worthing WOW's celebration of film in Sussex, in 2016 they worked with Heritage Trail App developer, Echoes, to create two audio trails. These trails of Worthing and Shoreham take you to key locations with a cinematic link. You can download it for free from the App Store – search for Worthing WOW.

Worthing

The Dome Cinema, BN11 3PT
Film: *Wish You were Here*

The pier at Worthing, BN11 3PX
Films: *Wish You Were Here*, *The Rise and Rise of Michael Rimmer*, *Dance with a Stranger*, *Cor Blimey*, *The Fear*
First films screened in Worthing at the original Pavilion at the sea.

Marine Parade, BN11 3QG
Films: *Up the Junction*, *Dance with a Stranger*

Eriswell Road, BN11 3HP
Film: *The Birthday Party*

Plaza Cinema now Gala Bingo, **BN11 3JS**

Connaught Cinema, BN11 1LG

ELECTRIC PICTURES

York Road, BN11 3EN
Film: *Wish You Were Here*

Castle Tavern, Newland Road, **BN11 1JR**
Film: *Cuffs*

Chesswood Road, BN11 2AA
Film: *Wish You Were Here*

Southdown Garage, Library Place, **BN11 3EZ**
Film: *Wish You Were Here*

Splash Point
Film: *Wish You Were Here*

Worthing Town Hall, BN11 9SA
Film: *Cuffs*

Alfred Place, BN11 3EP
Film: *Wish You Were Here*

Rowlands Road, BN11 3JJ
Film: *Wish You Were Here*

Shoreham

Adur Civic Centre, BN43 6PR
Film: *Cuffs*: the interior of the location was used for holding cell scenes and for the office-set scenes.

Shoreham Fort, BN43 5HY
Site of the Sunny South Film Company 1914–15
Film: *The Battle of the V1*

Church of the Good Shepherd, BN43 5LG
Site of Sealight studio, later used by Progress and Walter West

Shoreham Harbour, BN42 4ED
Films: *Rogue's Yarn, Ghost Ship*

Shoreham Airport, BN43 5FF

Films: *Body Stealers, Richard III, Poirot (three episodes), The Da Vinci Code, Woman in Gold, The Crown*

Kingston Bay Road, BN43 5HP

Film: *The Flaw*

Quarry and cliff top at Truleigh Hill, just outside Shoreham, BN43 5FB

Film: *Hell Drivers*

The beach at Shoreham (seafront)

Film: *The Battle of the V1*

Gardner Road, BN41 1PN

Film: *Smokescreen*

18

FILMOGRAPHY OF WORTHING, LANCING AND SHOREHAM, 1898-2015

Seven actuality films (filmed 6–7 April 1898)
Three survive in full at the BFI National Archive, with one (water polo match) available to view via BFI Screenonline

A Nurse's Devotion (1912)
A 'lost' film

The Motor Bandits (1912)
Survives in full at Screen Archive South East

Building a Chicken House (1914)
A 'lost' film

The Jockey (1914)
A 'lost' film

Moving a Piano (1914)
A 'lost' film

The Showman's Dream (1914)
A 'lost' film

Tincture of Iron (1914)
A 'lost' film

Will Evans' Comedies (1914)
A 'lost' film

Some Fun (1915)
A 'lost' film

A Study in Skarlit (1915)
A 'lost' film

A Man and a Woman (1916)
A 'lost' film

A Man's Shadow (1920)
A 'lost' film

By Berwyn Banks (1920)
A 'lost' film

FILMOGRAPHY

Lady Noggs (1920)
A 'lost' film

Little Dorrit (1920)
Fragment survives in Screen Archive
South East

Sweet and Twenty (1920)
A 'lost' film

The Black Sheep (1920)
A 'lost' film

The Children of Gibeon (1920)
A 'lost' film

The Scarlet Wooing (1920)
A 'lost' film

Two Little Wooden Shoes (1920)
A 'lost' film

A Lowland Cinderella (1921)
Survives in full at Screen Archive
South East

Moth and Rust (1921)
A 'lost' film

The Mayor of Casterbridge (1921)
Fragment survives in Screen Archive
South East

The Woman of the Iron Bracelets (1921)
A 'lost' film

The Lilac Sunbonnet (1922)
A 'lost' film

Fires of Innocence (1923)
Survives in full at the BFI National Archive

Little Miss Nobody (1923)
A 'lost' film

Rogues on the Turf (1923)
A 'lost' film

Hornet's Nest (1924)
A 'lost' film

Was She Justified? (1924)
A 'lost' film

Ghost Ship (1952)
Available on DVD: Classic Horror
Collection, 2007

The Floating Dutchman (1952)
Available on DVD: label unknown, year
unknown

Dangerous Voyage (1954)
Available on DVD: on the Network
label, 2014

The Flaw (1955)
Available on DVD: on the Renown
label, 2013

Rogue's Yarn (1957)
Available on DVD: on the Renown
label, 2015

Battle of the V1 (1958)
Available on DVD: on the Renown label
(in colour), 2012

Smokescreen (1964)
Available on DVD: on the Renown
label, 2012

The Birthday Party (1968)
Available on DVD: on the Fremantle label, 2001

Up the Junction (1968)
Available on DVD: on the Paramount Home Entertainment label, 2008

The Body Stealers (aka *Invasion of the Body Stealers* & *Thin Air*) (1969)
Available on DVD: on the Odeon Entertainment label, 2011

The Rise and Rise of Michael Rimmer (1970)
Available on DVD: on the Digital Classics label, 2007

Dance with a Stranger (1985)
Available on DVD: on the Channel 4 label, 2007

Wish You Were Here (1987)
Available on DVD: on the Channel 4 label, 2007

Poirot, 'The Adventure of the Western Star' (1990)
Available on DVD: on the Cinema Club label, 2003

Poirot, 'Death in the Clouds' (1992)
Available on DVD: label unknown

Resort to Murder (TV series) (1995)
No DVD listing available

Richard III (1995)
Available on DVD: on the BFI label, 2016

Men Behaving Badly, 'Gary in Love' (1998)
DVD available as part of the Complete Collection boxed set: on the Fremantle Home Entertainment label, 2012

Cor, Blimey! (2000) (single TV drama)
Available on DVD: label unknown, 2000 (US import)

Poirot, 'Lord Edgware Dies' (2000)
No DVD listing available

The Da Vinci Code (2006)
Available on DVD: on the Sony Pictures Home Entertainment label, 2006

Brideshead Revisited (2008)
Available on DVD: on the BBC 2 Entertain label, 2009

The Fear (2012) (TV series)
Available on DVD: on the BBC label, year unavailable

Black Sea (2015)
Available on DVD: on the Universal Pictures UK label, 2015

Cuffs (2015) (TV series)
Available on DVD: on the Spirit Entertainment Limited label, 2016

Woman in Gold (2015)
Available on DVD: on the Entertainment in Video label, 2015

FURTHER READING

Colquhoun, Edward & Alice, *Hollywood-By-Sea: A pictorial chronicle of Bungalow Town, Shoreham-by-Sea* (self-published, 2013)

Eyles, Gray and Readman, *Cinema West Sussex: The First Hundred Years* (Phillimore & Co. 1996)

Fisher, David, *Cinema by Sea: Film and Cinema in Brighton & Hove Since 1896* (Terra Media Ltd, 2012)

Huntley, John, *Silver Screen, Silent Voices: The story of film-making at Bungalow Town – Shoreham Beach 1914–1923* (DVD, South East Film and Video Archive. Published in the UK by Cinemedia in association with the South East Film and Video Archive, 2008)

Payne, John, *Notes and Memories on Filmmaking at Bungalow Town, Shoreham Beach 1914–1923* (self-published, 2015)

West Sussex on the Silver Screen: Films Made in West Sussex during the first 100 years of cinema (West Sussex County Council, 1995)

Wilmer, John, *Full Circle: The story of Worthing's Connaught Theatre* (Optimus Books, 1999)

Wolters, Neb, *Bungalow Town: Theatre & Film Colony* (Marlipins Museum, 1995, 2nd edition)

The History Press